T0007040

Is Our Food Killing Us?

The Big Idea

Joy Manning

Is Our Food Killing Us?

A primer for the 21st century

Over 180 illustrations

General Editor:
Matthew Taylor

Contents

Introduction   6

1. The Evolution of an Epidemic   20

2. The Health Hazards of Processed Food   46

3. The Dark Side of Industrial Food   78

4. Back to Health   102

Conclusion   128

Further Reading   136

Picture Credits   138

Index   140

Acknowledgments   144

Introduction

A

If there is one thing with the power to unite us as human beings, it is food. Regardless of how different individuals and groups may be from one another, everyone has to eat. Food is among our most basic biological needs. But we all know it is more than fuel.

Food is a way to bond with our families and communities, and to forge new connections with other cultures. It can be sentimental, nostalgic and romantic. Cooking and eating is a form of self-expression; food choices are a political act. We use food to signal our own identities and value systems: 'I don't eat meat', or 'I'm a meat and potatoes kind of a guy', as well as to assign identity to others.

Food is ceremonial, religious, traditional and tribal. In fact, it is one of those aspects of life that looms so large it can become invisible. Dietary patterns and eating habits can be automatic and go unexamined for years, decades or an entire lifetime.

But there is every reason to take a step back and ask ourselves questions about what we eat and why. As often as you have heard the cliché, 'You are what you eat', if you are anything like most people, you have not internalized this wisdom.

A   Food is central to culture around the world. Here, a family shares stories over lunch during the Magallanes district fiesta in the Philippines. The fiesta is an annual celebration during which food plays a central part. Families gather for a large lunch of Lechon, a style of roast pork.

B   Volunteers serve free Thanksgiving meals during the annual 'Safeway Feast of Sharing' in Washington, D.C. The event has fed more than 70,000 people since 1999, providing people in need with a vital link to a significant cultural event in the US.

C   Meals are laid out on the first day of Ramadan at the shrine of Hazrat Nizamuddin Aulia, a 13th-century Sufi Muslim saint, in New Delhi, India. Throughout the holy month devout Muslims fast until after sunset, when they break the fast with a meal known as Iftar.

INTAKE OF DIETARY FACTORS AMONG ADULTS AGED ≥ 25 WORLDWIDE (2017)

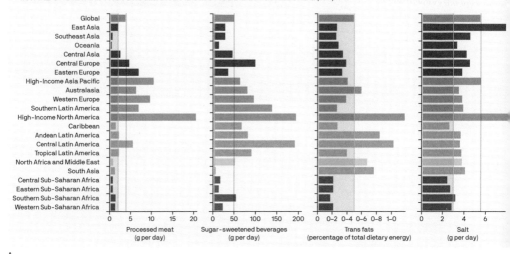

A

Thanks to advances in medicine, people do not die from many of the things that used to kill us frequently 100 years ago. In the early 1900s, the most common causes of death were diseases like pneumonia, tuberculosis and diphtheria. Now these illnesses are either nearly eradicated or highly treatable.

Today, some of the most common causes of preventable deaths include heart disease, diabetes, cancer and stroke. In 2017 the Global Burden of Disease study found that a poor diet was the highest risk factor for early death worldwide, responsible for 10.9 million deaths. The second highest risk factor was high blood pressure (itself, determined in part by diet), which caused 10.4 million deaths, and the third highest was tobacco, causing 8 million.

Heart disease, or cardio-vascular disease, refers to the blocked arteries that cause heart attacks and strokes. It is the world's biggest killer, but it is 80 per cent preventable.

Diabetes occurs when either the pancreas does not make enough insulin (Type 1) or the body does not react as it should to insulin (Type 2). Both types cause a dangerous rise in blood sugar.

Cancer is a blanket term for diseases characterized by abnormal cell division. There are more than 100 types, but some of the most common include lung, breast and skin cancer.

A **stroke** occurs when the brain is deprived of blood, and therefore deprived of oxygen as well. It is compared to a heart attack and sometimes called a 'brain attack'.

High blood pressure is excess force placed on blood vessels. It increases your risk of heart disease but often has no symptoms.

The **Industrial Revolution**, *c.* 1760–1830, was the transition from a largely agrarian economy to one dominated by power-driven machines. It fundamentally changed farming and manufacturing.

A   This chart shows the age-standardized intake of processed meat, sugar-sweetened beverages, trans fats and salt among adults aged 25 years or older in 2017. Intake is shown at both the global and regional level. It demonstrates the problems of the modern Western diet, and how extensively it has been exported around the world.

Our food is killing us. And that is at least partially because we let it.

But it is not all personal gluttony that is to blame for the skyrocketing rates of obesity and diabetes. The forces that shape what we eat transcend the individual. They are largely driven by politics, policies, the needs and whims of multinational mega corporations and, most of all, money. The massive changes to agriculture brought about by the Industrial Revolution set off changes to our food supply that continue to affect the way we eat today.

When most people imagine a farm, they call to mind weathered red barns, lush green pastures and fluffy, happy chickens clucking in the sunshine. It is a relaxing, pleasant scene. And of course, behind it is the family who has cultivated this patch of land for generations. They produce meat, milk, eggs and a variety of vegetables for themselves and their community. Sounds nice, right? It is the kind of place you would love to support with the money in your food budget and perhaps even visit one day.

Unfortunately, in the industrialized West this traditional family farm is now little more than an historic artefact. In the early 1900s, an era considered by many to be farming's heyday, the United States was home to more than 6 million farms, most of them of the small, family-run type you might still think of when you imagine farming today. More than half of Americans were farmers or lived in a farming community. By 2012, the number of US farms had fallen to 2 million, while the overall area of land being farmed remained the same. Between 2005 and 2016 the number of farms in the European Union decreased by one quarter, and again the land used for agricultural production stayed broadly unchanged.

In developed nations, agriculture is increasingly dominated by large, corporate farms. You may have heard them referred to as factory farms, a term that correctly suggests these operations are more concerned with scale, profit and efficiency than responsible stewardship of the land or the health of their communities. Big Food is now a massive multi-industry that produces and sells the vast majority of what we eat and shapes eating behaviour across the planet with the irresistible ultra-processed foods it churns out and the relentless advertising that comes with them.

A

Factory farms are large industrialized farms. Livestock on such farms are often overcrowded, overmedicated and subject to inhumane conditions.

Big Food is an informal term used to describe the corporate domination of our food supplies. It covers factory farms, large food companies and powerful industry lobbyists.

Ultra-processed foods are packaged and fast foods that bear little resemblance to whole foods. They are high in refined sugar, flour and fat and typically contain many additives and preservatives.

B

C

In the developing world the picture is different. In Asia and sub-Saharan Africa 80 per cent of food is produced by smallholder farmers, and in 2011 in South Asia the average farm size was just 1.4 hectares (in the US it was 178.4 hectares). However, even these countries are not beyond the reach of factory farming. It is on the rise everywhere. A 2017 study by the John's Hopkins Centre for a Livable Future on food production in low- and middle-income countries found that while factory farming is not yet dominant, it is a growing trend, and national government policies tend to favour growth and industrialization in animal farming.

How did this transformation happen?

Mechanization played a large role. As with other segments of the economy during this time, tasks that once required manual labour, and lots of it, were taken over by machines, such as the seed drill and threshing machine. No longer were people milking cows, picking vegetables, sorting eggs or sowing seeds by hand or with the help of animal labour.

This shift greatly improved agricultural efficiency, making it possible to produce larger amounts of grains and seeds quickly and cheaply. It was hailed as a necessary innovation, a way to scale up food production to feed more people as population growth exploded. Between 1950 and the late 1960s the Green Revolution, or Third Agricultural Revolution, increased worldwide agricultural production again, through new technologies including chemical fertilizers, agrochemicals and high-yielding varieties (HYVs) of cereals. These revolutions changed the workforce and the food supply forever. In 1900, 41 per cent of Americans worked in agriculture. By the year 2000, it was only 2 per cent.

Technology also brought chemicals. Traditionally, fields were fertilized with compost and manure produced mostly on the farm itself, while pests were managed by natural means. Today, manufactured synthetic fertilizers and pesticides dominate – innovations that dramatically improved crop yields but brought serious troubles of their own.

The **Green Revolution** was the mid-20th-century boom in grain production. It was brought about by the introduction of high-yield varieties of grain.

High-yielding varieties (HYVs) are agricultural crops that have been carefully bred or genetically modified to maximize the quantity of food harvested.

Fertilizers are any natural or artificial substance applied to crops with the intention of increasing the yield by returning nitrogen or carbon to the soil.

Pesticides are any natural or artificial substance applied to crops to minimize animals, insects or other pests that inhibit crop growth.

Antibiotics are medicines that work in people and animals to combat bacterial illness. They are also used to promote rapid weight gain in livestock. This practice has contributed to antibiotic resistance.

The **World Health Organization (WHO)** is an agency of the United Nations that works on a wide variety of international health initiatives.

And then, of course, there are the drugs. Antibiotics benefit big agriculture in multiple ways. For one thing, routine dosing with these medications allows pigs, cows and chickens to grow fatter faster, and on less feed. It also helps animals survive the crowded, unhealthy conditions that they must endure on factory farms.

A   An overhead view of farmers spraying pesticide on a field of rice in Huaian, Jiangsu province, China. Pesticides continue to be a serious issue in China, where their use has increased dramatically. Pesticide use in China is estimated to be 1.5 to 4 times larger than the global average.

Pesticides, antibiotics and other technological advancements that helped pave the way for industrial farms have turned out not to be the miracles early nineteenth-century farmers probably thought they were. The World Health Organization (WHO) notes that pesticides are potentially toxic to humans and can have both acute and chronic health effects. Many people have long tried to avoid exposure to them. Certain pesticides remain in the soil and water for years after they were initially applied; many dangerous pesticides have been banned in developed countries but remain in widespread use in developing countries throughout the world. The insecticide monocrotophos is banned in the EU and US but is still available in India, and in 2013 it caused the deaths of 23 children when their school lunch was contaminated.

A

In the heyday of family farms, people ate much less meat than we do today. Producing meat was more expensive in the days before ubiquitous automation, and it was therefore much more of a luxury good. Modern, large-scale meat production 'farms', commonly called concentrated animal feeding operations (CAFOs), have made meat much less expensive and more widely available.

There is a clear link between wealth and meat consumption however, as wealthier countries eat far more meat than poorer ones. In 2013 Americans ate more than 100 kilograms (220 lb) of meat per person annually, whilst in Nigeria the average was just 9 kilograms (19 lb) per person. Culture and history also have an impact, as in India, where vegetarianism has been popular since the introduction of Buddhism and Jainism in the 6th century BCE, 38 per cent of the population are vegetarian. However, thanks to the current abundant meat and dairy supply, globally we eat more meat than ever before, even as we learn more about how this meat-rich, high-calorie, high-saturated fat diet is one of the main drivers of heart disease, claiming more than 15 million lives around the world each year.

A

B

Concentrated animal feeding operations (CAFOs) are industrial-scale livestock facilities where hundreds, or even tens of thousands, of animals are raised in overcrowded and inhumane conditions.

Carcinogenic describes any substance known to promote cancer. Examples include tobacco, alcohol and processed meat.

High fructose corn syrup (HFCS) is a corn-derived sweetener in which glucose has been converted to fructose. It is a common ingredient in ultra-processed food.

A   A scene from a typical CAFO, or concentrated animal feeding operation. Here, pigs eat from a feeder in Howard County, Iowa. CAFOs like this often pollute surrounding areas.
B   Turkey farming places a premium on breeding birds rapidly and for large breast size, which is prized by consumers. This turkey farm in Turkey shows a typically overcrowded growing operation in which the birds have little to no outdoor access.
C   An employee monitors stacks of sliced ham as it comes off the production line at a facility in China. The plant imports pork from the US, and manufactures products designed to meet the growing demand for American-style processed meat in China.
D   Sugary candy canes are a mainstay of the holiday season. Here, the highly processed treats are being made from candy cane scraps and corn syrup at a factory in Denver, Colorado.

C

D

Processed meats – a way to use salt, chemicals and preservatives to make a highly perishable foodstuff more shelf stable – are so damaging to our health that they are considered carcinogenic by the World Health Organization.

In fact, most of the fruits of factory farming, meat or vegetable, do no favours for human health. Wholesome wheat is stripped of its most nutritious parts before being refined and turned into nutritionally bankrupt (but highly profitable and shelf-stable) foods such as pizza dough, white bread and breakfast cereals. Soybeans are squeezed for their oil, which is then used for deep fat frying, yielding an abundance of ultra-processed convenience food. Corn becomes high fructose corn syrup (HFCS), a cheap sugar substitute that many experts believe is largely responsible for the obesity crisis. One reason for this is HFCS is cheaper than the cane sugar used before it, so sweetened products could become cheaper or bigger. Another is that because the body metabolizes fructose differently to regular sugar it converts to fat more quickly, and inhibits the production of leptin, the satiety-inducing hormone.

A

A An industrial milk packaging line at a dairy farm in the Ryazan region, Russia.

B In Delhi, India, corporate giant McDonald's delivers fast food via mopeds. India's first McDonald's opened in 1996, and the restaurants there have an adapted menu to cater to Indian customs and culture. They serve no beef or pork, instead offering alternative products such as the Chicken Maharajah Mac and Aloo Tikki Burger. In 2012 McDonald's opened its first vegetarian-only restaurant in India.

Biodiversity loss refers to a decrease in the overall number of living species of plants and animals.

As farming transforms from a traditional, agrarian way of life to profit-driven factory farms run by corporate CEOs living far away from the communities where the food is produced, the food supply itself changes. Food culture changes. What we eat – and how much of it – is very different from what it used to be wherever the typical modern Western diet is exported around the world. A revolution that was supposed to make life and the global food system better actually set in motion changes that have made the food we eat, and our health, markedly worse.

Policy makers at local and national levels impact our food environment, for example with programmes that reward farmers for growing more and more corn, or taxes that hit consumers in their wallets when they buy sugary soda. All these forces and more are brought to bear on your dinner plate.

B

There is a rising awareness that the typical modern Western diet (now exported globally and increasingly popular in industrialized countries worldwide) while great for multinational corporations, is terrible for public health. It is driving the preventable, chronic diseases that are taking lives in great numbers. Just as tragically, the global food system is responsible for a quarter of the world's total greenhouse gas emissions, and contributes to biodiversity loss, water pollution and the global plastic crisis. As the world population continues to grow, and the food system attempts to expand further, damage to the ecosystem will only increase: a fundamental change in approach is required.

Understanding the complex issues surrounding dietary patterns can be the first step to taking the political actions necessary. Voting for leaders who support more human-centred food and farming policies, and who encourage the development of new cultivated meat and other food-creation technologies, is also key to shifting these disturbing trends in a positive direction.

1. The Evolution of an Epidemic

A

Obesity is a global health crisis, and for years it has been referred to as an epidemic.

A   In China, where childhood obesity has become more common, many middle class parents send their kids to summer camps geared toward fitness and weight loss, like this one in Beijing.

B   Body mass index is calculated by dividing a person's weight by their height squared. This chart makes it easy to find your BMI number from your height and weight, and to see which weight range it falls into.

Increasingly, medical professionals around the world have adopted a disease model of obesity. Thinking of obesity as an illness makes sense in many ways. During the past several decades, obesity has skyrocketed and its health consequence cannot be denied. And not just in the rich countries where you might expect it to be high. It has become a problem across the globe. According to a report from the World Health Organization, 650 million adults are obese. That rate is twice as high as it was 50 years ago. Worldwide, obesity has increased threefold since 1974.

Obesity is defined as having a body mass index (commonly known as BMI, a measure of body size that factors in both weight and height) of more than 30. BMI is an imperfect tool for assessing a person's health, but it does tell a story about the health risks of obesity, especially when you study, as epidemiologists do, groups of people instead of individuals.

Body mass index is an estimation of body fat based on a ratio of height to weight.

With more people living with obesity than ever, it should come as no surprise that there is a forceful movement around the idea of fat acceptance. With its roots in 1960s activism, and informed by the feminist and gay rights campaigns of the 1970s, the movement fights for an end to prejudice against fat people. Despite this, overweight and obese people continue to face discrimination in all areas of life. This is especially pronounced when it comes to getting medical care. All too often, doctors want to place the blame for unrelated health conditions on a patient's weight.

B

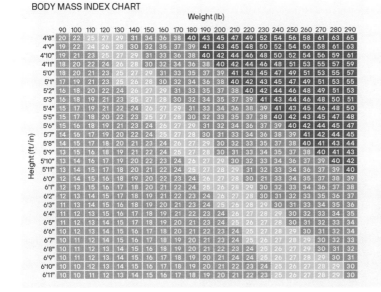

BODY MASS INDEX CHART

Height (ft/in) \ Weight (lb)	90	100	110	120	130	140	150	160	170	180	190	200	210	220	230	240	250	260	270	280	290
4'8"	20	22	25	27	29	31	34	36	38	40	43	45	47	49	52	54	56	58	61	63	65
4'9"	19	22	24	26	28	30	32	35	37	39	41	43	45	48	50	52	54	56	58	61	63
4'10"	19	21	23	25	27	29	31	33	36	38	40	42	44	46	48	50	52	54	56	59	61
4'11"	18	20	22	24	26	28	30	32	34	36	38	40	42	44	46	48	51	53	55	57	59
5'0"	18	20	21	23	25	27	29	31	33	35	37	39	41	43	45	47	49	51	53	55	57
5'1"	17	19	21	23	25	26	28	30	32	34	36	38	40	42	43	45	47	49	51	53	55
5'2"	16	18	20	22	24	26	27	29	31	33	35	37	38	40	42	44	46	48	49	51	53
5'3"	16	18	19	21	23	25	27	28	30	32	34	35	37	39	41	43	44	46	48	50	51
5'4"	15	17	19	21	22	24	26	27	29	31	33	34	36	38	39	41	43	45	46	48	50
5'5"	15	17	18	20	22	23	25	27	28	30	32	33	35	37	38	40	42	43	45	47	48
5'6"	15	16	18	19	21	23	24	26	27	29	31	32	34	36	37	39	40	42	44	45	47
5'7"	14	16	17	19	20	22	24	25	27	28	30	31	33	34	36	38	39	41	42	44	45
5'8"	14	15	17	18	20	21	23	24	26	27	29	30	32	33	35	37	38	40	41	43	44
5'9"	13	15	16	18	19	21	22	24	25	27	28	30	31	33	34	35	37	38	40	41	43
5'10"	13	14	16	17	19	20	22	23	24	26	27	29	30	32	33	34	36	37	39	40	42
5'11"	13	14	15	17	18	20	21	22	24	25	27	28	29	31	32	33	34	36	37	39	40
6'0"	12	14	15	16	18	19	20	22	23	24	26	27	28	30	21	33	34	35	37	38	39
6'1"	12	13	15	16	17	18	20	21	22	24	25	26	28	29	30	32	33	34	36	37	38
6'2"	12	13	14	15	17	18	19	21	22	23	24	26	27	28	30	31	32	33	35	36	37
6'3"	11	13	14	15	16	18	19	20	21	23	24	25	26	28	29	30	31	33	34	35	36
6'4"	11	12	13	15	16	17	18	19	20	21	23	24	25	26	27	28	30	31	32	33	34
6'5"	11	12	13	14	15	17	18	19	20	21	23	24	25	26	27	28	30	31	32	33	34
6'6"	10	12	13	14	15	16	17	18	20	21	22	23	24	25	26	27	28	29	30	31	32
6'7"	10	11	12	13	14	15	16	18	19	20	21	22	23	24	25	26	27	28	29	32	33
6'8"	10	11	12	13	14	15	16	17	18	19	20	21	22	23	24	25	26	27	29	30	32
6'9"	10	11	12	13	13	14	15	16	17	18	19	20	21	24	24	25	26	27	28	29	31
6'10"	10	11	12	13	14	15	16	17	18	19	20	21	22	23	25	26	27	28	29	30	30
6'11"	10	10	11	12	13	14	15	16	17	18	19	20	21	22	23	25	26	27	28	29	30

Underweight
BMI = less than 18.5

Normal weight
BMI = 18.5 to 24.9

Overweight
BMI = 25 to 29.9

Obese
BMI = 30 to 39.9

Extremely obese
BMI = 40 and above

A   As the fat acceptance movement has gained traction, so have plus sized fashion influencers such as Virginie Grossat, who has tens of thousands of followers on social media.

B   As the prevalence of obesity grows, more large people embrace and celebrate their size with fat positive events and apparel.

Weight bias in medicine is a well-documented problem, and it can lead to overweight and obese patients avoiding medical care. A 2012 study published in *Obesity Research* found that even medical professionals working in the area of obesity view fat individuals as more lazy, stupid and worthless than thin people, and a 2018 review by A. Tomiyama, Deborah Carr, Ellen Granberg *et al* of nearly 70 studies on weight stigma found that it actually led people to eat more. Fat acceptance and 'health at every size' advocates raise awareness around these important issues, with the goal of making health care comfortable and accessible to all.

At the same time, the scientific evidence that obesity on the population level increases the risk of myriad health problems is overwhelming. Elevated BMIs increase the risks for the deadliest chronic health problems, including heart disease and diabetes. A study conducted by the Institute for Health Metrics and Evaluation at the University of Washington, USA, found that in 2015 having a high BMI accounted for 4 million deaths worldwide. According to Cancer Research UK being overweight or obese is the second biggest preventable cause of cancer in the UK.

A

Weight bias refers to the attitudes that cause discrimination against people who are overweight or obese. It is an especially serious problem in health care.

Metabolically healthy means attaining target levels of blood glucose, blood lipids, blood pressure and waist circumference without the use of drugs.

B

Some experts claim that obese people who engage in healthy lifestyle behaviours, such as regular exercise, can be fat and fit at the same time. A 2004 study published in *The Journal of the American Medical Association* by cardiologist C. Noel Bairey-Merz found fitness was more relevant than weight when it came to women protecting themselves from heart disease. While it is always better for your health to be active than it is to be sedentary, a 2018 study published in *The Lancet* indicates the opposite: that even metabolically healthy people who are overweight are at a higher risk for heart attacks, heart failures and strokes than healthy weight people who are also metabolically healthy.

In spite of the serious health risks that come with obesity, it only became formally recognized as a disease in the United States by the American Medical Association relatively recently, in 2013. It was hoped that reframing the condition this way would combat weight bias. A disease diagnosis can change the conversation from one about laziness, poor self-control around food or personal responsibility to one about health and healing. Recognizing obesity as a chronic, relapsing, progressive disease is especially important to those for whom weight management is a genetic problem. Some experts estimate that this could range from 40 to 70 per cent of cases.

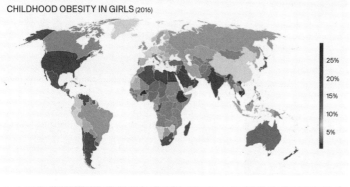

CHILDHOOD OBESITY IN GIRLS (2016)

25%
20%
15%
10%
5%

CHILDHOOD OBESITY IN BOYS (2016)

25%
20%
15%
10%
5%

A

A These colour-coded maps show the prevalence of childhood obesity in both boys and girls around the world. The percentage of children that are obese is indicated using the colour scale.

B This Colombian eight-year-old weighs 90 kg (198 lb) – more than three times her ideal weight. Here, her mother helps at a medical checkup.

The US is not alone in its position that obesity is a disease. Canada, Portugal, the World Health Organization and the World Obesity Federation all classify obesity in this way. And there is a push among medical associations and organizations in many other countries around the world, including the UK, to officially recognize obesity as a disease. Doing so could help clear a path for the establishment of treatment, help patients pay for care and lead to greater research funding.

Perhaps because of obesity's very recent classification as a disease, doctors have not historically been well trained on the subject of nutrition. And during a routine surgery visit, they usually have very limited time – 10 or 15 minutes – to spend with a patient. As the idea of obesity as a disease takes hold, the hope is that treatments, including nutrition education and behaviour modification techniques, will be refined and become a more standard part of medical treatment plans.

Childhood obesity is described by the World Health Organization as one of the most serious public health challenges of the 21st century. This problem is especially dire in developing countries, which have a rate of childhood obesity 30 per cent higher than in developed countries.

Type 2 diabetes was long known as 'adult-onset' diabetes because it was a disease of middle-aged and older adults, rarely seen in children. Thanks to the global food system, youth-onset type 2 diabetes is rising at an alarming rate, setting young people up for a lifetime of ill health. Though genetics also plays a role, type 2 diabetes is associated with excess weight, poor diet and lack of exercise.

B

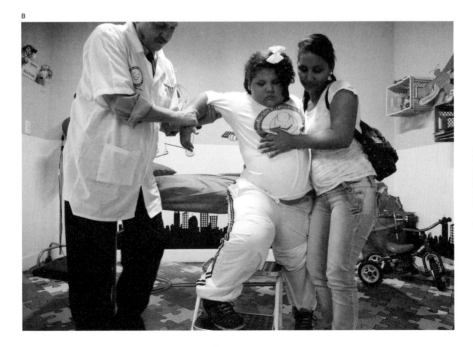

Of course, the rise of obesity did not happen in a vacuum. The way people grow, make and distribute food has changed as dramatically as human waistlines. The evolution of the food system from a web of independent family farms to the factory farm model also known as 'big agriculture' has changed much more than the business and practice of farming. Its ripple effects totally transformed the food system by flooding the economy with cheap commodity crops that could readily be transformed into a spectacular range of new foodstuffs.

America led the way in this regard. Perhaps because the United States was such a young country at the time of those sweeping changes to agriculture, the shift to highly processed and manufactured food was enthusiastically embraced. Canned foods were marvels of convenience. When they arrived, frozen TV dinners were, thanks in part to massive advertising campaigns, regarded as not only a treat but a way to liberate women from the domestic drudgery of cooking from scratch. It could also be America's lack of a single unifying food culture – featuring as it does the influence of numerous immigrant communities and a vast array of regional specialities – that made the country so eager to adopt an entirely new type of diet. Countries that have stuck closer to their traditional healthy food cultures, such as Italy and Japan, have fared better than America when it comes to obesity rates.

A

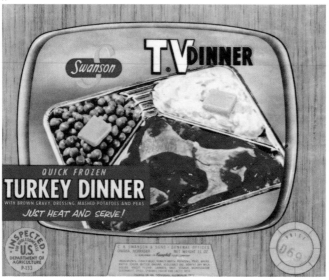

A Swanson's 1954 'TV dinner', designed to resemble a television set and encourage the new dining habits made possible by technological innovation.
B The original White Castle restaurant in Wichita, Kansas. In 2014, *Time* magazine named its slider the most influential burger of all time.
C The first McDonald's in California opened in 1940. The famous golden arches were not introduced until 1953.

Big agriculture (or Big Ag) is a negative phrase used to describe modern industrial farming and the problems associated with it.

Standard American Diet (SAD) or Western diet refers to a pattern of eating that is high in meat, saturated fat, refined flour and sugar, while low in vegetables and fibre.

B

C

And of course, it was America that gave birth to fast food when the original White Castle hamburger chain opened in 1921. By 1940, McDonald's was on the scene, followed by KFC in 1952. By some estimates, there are a quarter of a million fast food restaurants in the United States. Today, one in three American adults eats fast food every day. It is a cornerstone of what is commonly called the Standard American Diet (SAD) or Western diet.

This eating pattern is characterized by an abundance of fast food and other highly processed food. It is full of refined sugars and saturated fat from meat and dairy. Vegetables, whole grains, legumes, fibre and fruit are conspicuously absent.

A

The **North American Free Trade Agreement** is a 1994 agreement between the United States, Canada and Mexico intended to promote trade between the countries and eliminate tariffs.

The **World Trade Organization** is an international group focusing on global trade rules in an effort to make global trading run smoothly.

Slow Food is a movement founded in Italy in 1989, but now active worldwide, to promote local foodways, sustainable farming, and traditional recipes and styles of cooking. The name is meant to oppose fast food.

This is the diet that has contributed to America's well-documented and deadly obesity problem. Unfortunately, this diet has also become one of America's most popular exports. A complex web of agricultural, trade, marketing and scientific practices – many of which were initially designed to benefit the US in international markets – are helping to drive the global obesity epidemic.

Mexico, for instance, was flooded with cheap junk food and soda following the 1994 passage of the North American Free Trade Agreement. As a result, obesity has spiked in the country, and when the Mexican government tried to tax drinks containing high fructose corn syrup Washington complained to the World Trade Organization and the tax was struck down. McDonald's sells burgers, fries and shakes at more than 34,000 locations in 118 countries around the world, and Coca-Cola and PepsiCo control almost 40 per cent of the world's $53 billion soft drinks market, according to *The Economist*.

Globalization, trade deals and increasing urbanization have contributed to the rapid rise of the Western diet globally. In places where well established food cultures exist, such as Italy, there has been a measure of resistance to the incursion of mass-produced, processed food.

A In 2018 President Donald Trump invited NCAA football national champions, the Clemson Tigers, to the White House for a banquet of fast food from Domino's, McDonald's, Wendy's and Burger King.

B Over 38,000 McDonald's restaurants may be found in more than 100 countries around the world. Here they are seen in India (above left) and China (above and below right). Their success has also inevitably prompted knock-off versions, such as 'Mash Donald's' in Tehran, Iran (below left).

The Slow Food organization, which advocates for the preservation of traditional food ways, was famously founded after Italy's first McDonald's opened in Rome in 1986. Though Italy's population on average remains thinner than most other countries in Europe, its rate of obesity has climbed since the introduction of the Standard American Diet. This trend is particularly prevalent among children, with the Organization for Economic Co-operation and Development (OECD) reporting in 2014 that 36 per cent of boys and 34 per cent of girls under 18 were obese, giving Italy the second highest rates of childhood obesity in the world (after Greece). The Western diet has also spread to developing countries and is driving up obesity in those places, as well as the chronic diseases that go along with it, like diabetes. It is estimated that two thirds of people living with obesity around the world live in developing countries.

B

An instructive example comes from Samoa. Turkey tails, which can be up to 40 per cent fat, are largely an unwanted by-product of the US poultry industry. However, a clever marketing strategy following World War II led to them becoming a major export to the Pacific island of Samoa, which enjoyed close economic ties with the US at the time. By 2007 Samoans were each consuming an average of 20 kilograms (44 lb) of turkey tails per year, and unsurprisingly from the 1960s onwards obesity also skyrocketed, reaching 56 per cent in 2008. Traditional, leaner foods in the local diet, such as seafood, were pushed out. Samoan officials banned turkey tail imports in 2007. However, the World Trade Organization blocked their application for membership until 2011, when they agreed to reallow turkey tail imports.

What America is really exporting is not Happy Meals, fries and fried chicken. It is illness, obesity and premature death. A 2019 study conducted by researchers Nita G. Forouhi and Nigel Unwin and published in *The Lancet* suggests that the Western diet was the underlying cause of one in five deaths around the world. That is roughly 11 million deaths per year.

Of course, no one's cause of death is recorded officially as 'obesity'. Heart attack, heart failure, stroke, diabetes and cancer are some of the life-threatening health conditions in which diet plays a major role. According to the National Institute of Health, excess body weight is the second leading cause of preventable death in the United States. Many experts count it as the first.

Here are some of the common chronic conditions that can be triggered by diet, and the role food plays in getting sick:

A   Royal Foods brand turkey tails. This by-product of the US poultry industry is exported in large quantities to Samoa, where it is in part responsible for a dramatic rise in obesity.

B   In this image, the white globs on each plate represents the saturated fat found in common meals. The white liquid in the glasses represents the empty calories in soda and alcohol.

Heart disease is the top killer all around the world, and eating patterns dramatically shape cardiovascular health. Eating too much saturated fat, found in abundance in meat and dairy products, drives up LDL cholesterol (known as 'bad' cholesterol), which is associated with heart disease. Many of the best-loved foods on the planet are full of the stuff.

B

Bacon and eggs   Steak   Soda   Alcohol   Hamburger and fries

A

A Onion rings, burgers, hot dogs, fried chicken, French fries and pizza are all unhealthy staples of the modern Western diet, now exported around the world.

B Few people who eat a modern Western diet get enough of the colourful vegetables associated with maintaining a healthy body weight.

For example, just 50 grams (2 oz) of cheese contains around 12 grams (⅖ oz) of saturated fat, the upper limit of what you should eat in an entire day according to the American Heart Association. In the Western diet that cheese often comes on top of a beef burger. Even a modest 230-gram (8-oz) burger will provide another 16 grams (⅗ oz) of saturated fat. And this is just part of one meal. Add in buttered toast and milk at breakfast, a yoghurt snack, another serving of meat for dinner and perhaps some ice cream for dessert and you have eaten more saturated fat in one day than you probably should have in a week.

And then there is the salt. A salt-rich diet can lead to or exacerbate hypertension. Hypertension, also called high blood pressure, is known as the 'silent killer' because it does not have recognizable signs or symptoms – you need to have your blood pressure checked to know what's going on. Even after it is known, only about half the people who are aware of their high blood pressure have it under control. Hypertension can lead to stroke.

B

Insulin is a hormone that reduces blood sugar by helping it into the cells of the body, where it can be used for energy.

Type 2 diabetes is another major killer with an underlying cause at least partially due to eating habits. One of the most significant risk factors for developing type 2 diabetes is being overweight. Excess adipose tissue (body fat) contributes to something called insulin resistance. When that happens, the hormone insulin is less able to do its job of moving sugar out of the blood, resulting in high blood sugar. In response, the pancreas churns out more and more insulin to do the job, wearing itself out over time.

The typical Western diet is rich in foods that spike blood sugar, such as sweets, hamburgers and soda. Full of added sugars and low in fibre, they are digested quickly by the body, destabilizing blood sugar and leading to hunger soon after eating. The same foods that can help prevent diabetes – high fibre, low-sugar vegetables, whole grains and beans – can also help manage and even reverse diabetes. It is no coincidence that these same foods are associated with lower body weight as well.

Cancer is another deadly illness where food can be an underlying cause. There is a lot still to learn about the relationship between obesity and various forms of cancer. But experts agree that obesity is a major risk factor for at least eight kinds of cancer, including endometrial, breast, ovarian, prostate, liver, gallbladder, kidney and colon. Extremely obese women are seven times more likely to get endometrial cancer compared to women with body mass indexes in the healthy range, according to the National Cancer Institute. Those who are overweight or obese are twice as likely to develop liver cancer.

A

B

A This advertisement by Cancer Research UK sought to help the public understand that obesity, like cigarettes, causes cancer.

B This public health announcement in Slough, UK, reminds people that obesity increases the risk of becoming seriously ill with COVID-19, and encourages weight loss as a way of protecting yourself from the virus.

Eating patterns that contribute to obesity, such as the Western diet, also tend to be very low in the foods that are known to provide some protection from cancer. Cancer Research UK recommends a diet rich in vegetables, whole grains and beans for reducing cancer risk. Just as important as what you do eat, is what you do not eat. Cancer Research UK recommends limiting processed meat, sugary beverages and alcohol.

In 2020, a global analysis conducted by the University of North Carolina suggested that being obese doubled the risk of needing hospital treatment from COVID-19, and increased the risk of dying from the disease by nearly 50 per cent. They suggested this could be due to the fact obese patients were more likely to suffer from other conditions, such as high blood pressure and diabetes. They also warned a vaccine could be less effective for overweight people, as current flu vaccines do not work as well for those with a BMI over 30. This has led to governments around the world renewing their efforts to combat rising levels of obesity.

A

An individual's diet, so connected to getting or avoiding these fatal diseases, is only partially the result of personal choice. Increasingly communities across the globe are living in obesogenic environments, which make choosing health-promoting foods difficult while making obesity-causing foods omnipresent, cheap and attractive.

An obesogenic environment is one that encourages poor food choices for the people who live in it. It is a built environment that makes it easy and cheap to swing through a drive-through to pick up a coffee drink and breakfast sandwich (a morning meal that clocks in at around 1,000 calories) at a fast food chain instead of having a more nutritious and less calorific coffee and oatmeal at home. It is the vending machines stocked with crisps and chocolate bars instead of apples, and the school lunches that are laden with refined flour and saturated fat.

A A family of Iraqui immigrants living in Arizona stop for fast food at In-N-Out Burger.
B A graph demonstrating the top ten sources of calories for low-income individuals. Socio-economically disadvantaged people may live in a food desert, making it harder to access healthy and nutritious food.

The obesogenic environ-ment is a problem for everyone living in urban areas of developed countries, but it hits socioeconomically disadvantaged communities and those living in food deserts especially hard. Food deserts are communities situated more than one mile from a grocery store.

An **obesogenic environment** is one in which social and cultural norms encourage poor eating habits that increase the risk of obesity.

A **food desert** is a neighbourhood without easy access to supermarkets or other sources of fresh, whole foods. The term was first officially used in 1995 by researchers in the Low Income Project Team of the UK's Nutrition Task Force.

People who live in these disadvantaged areas face challenges to healthy eating that more prosperous people do not have. For example, they are less likely to have cars to take them to a supermarket in another neighbourhood or town. Often, they are working multiple jobs with unpredictable schedules. Lack of time and energy is a formidable obstacle to shopping and cooking healthy foods.

B

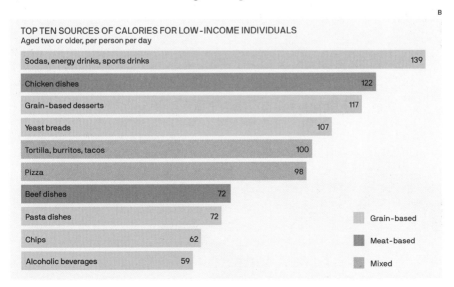

TOP TEN SOURCES OF CALORIES FOR LOW-INCOME INDIVIDUALS
Aged two or older, per person per day

Source	Value
Sodas, energy drinks, sports drinks	139
Chicken dishes	122
Grain-based desserts	117
Yeast breads	107
Tortilla, burritos, tacos	100
Pizza	98
Beef dishes	72
Pasta dishes	72
Chips	62
Alcoholic beverages	59

Grain-based
Meat-based
Mixed

Residents of food deserts often rely on the markets they do have: convenience stores. Access to these types of establishments increases the risk of obesity, as does the lack of a local supermarket. Convenience stores offer less fresh food, such as vegetables, and more processed foods, like shelf-stable crisps, crackers and snack cakes. Unfortunately, convenience stores are frequently located near schools, and kids who live in food deserts can develop the kind of eating patterns that lead to obesity at an early age.

Other aspects of the obesogenic environment cut across socio-economic lines. There is an assumption that poor people eat more fast food than those who are wealthy, but that is simply not true. A 2018 report from the Centers for Disease Control and Prevention (CDC) showed that, typically, the more money someone makes, the more fast food they eat. In varying degrees, the obesogenic environment affects everyone.

A

A Fast food giant KFC's notoriously unhealthy 'Double Down Dog' is a hotdog wrapped in fried chicken, instead of bread, and covered with cheese sauce.
B A staggering array of processed snacks for sale at a rest stop in Florida, USA. These cheap and unhealthy products are made easy and convenient to purchase by retailers.
C A wall of sugar-laden soft drinks for sale at a convenience shop in London, UK. The high level of sugar in these drinks not only encourages weight gain but is also bad for your teeth, as sugar feeds bacteria in your mouth, producing acid that leads to tooth decay.

B

C

But it is not just what we are eating that is killing us. It is also *how* we eat it. Food is part of a complex matrix of meals and behaviour. Feeling lonely, stressed, guilty or hurried can all influence how our food impacts our health. Diet intersects in meaningful ways with family, culture, community and mental health.

About half of all the meals and snacks adults eat in America are eaten alone, according to a report from the Food Marketing Institute. That is not so surprising when you consider that more people are living alone as well. In the EU one third of households have just one occupant, and in the United States more than a quarter do.

A

A Customers await a meal they will eat solo in partitioned booths at a chain restaurant in Tokyo, Japan, serving ramen noodles. Solo dining is a growing trend. In South Korea there is even a new word for it: *honbap*, a portmanteau of *honja* (alone), and *bap* (food).

Eating alone can contribute to overeating and weight gain in a few ways. Without company, you are more likely to try to multitask. Paying attention to your email inbox or the day's headlines will divert your attention from the experience of eating. These kinds of distractions make it all too easy to miss the subtle signals your body sends that you are full and it is time to stop eating. Solo diners may also eat too fast, without the breaks that are built in when you share a meal and conversation with someone else – you cannot chew and talk at the same time. The link between eating alone and weight gain was illustrated by a South Korean study published in *Obesity Research & Clinical Practice* in 2017, which found that for men eating alone was associated with a 45 per cent increased risk of being obese.

Those who eat alone are also far less likely to go through the hassle of cooking for themselves, so they will call for delivery, receiving the typical super-sized restaurant portion, or eat some other kind of processed convenience food. Pretty much all food prepared away from home is higher in calories and lower in nutrition than meals you make for yourself, as restaurant meals tend to have larger portion sizes, more saturated fat and salt and fewer vegetables. Indeed, the National Health and Nutrition Examination Survey found that less than 0.1 per cent of restaurant meals in the US were of an 'ideal quality', as defined by the American Heart Association.

The pace of modern life makes eating on the go – whether you are rushing from meeting to meeting or foraging for food in an airport terminal – inevitable for many. It is hard to find healthy options out there in the obesogenic environment, so eating on the go often adds up to eating junk food.

It has not always been this way. Before highly processed products came to dominate our food supply, when life had a slower pace, meals cooked from scratch and shared as a family were a daily ritual for many people around the world. These customs still exist. The French are more likely than Americans to share communal meals according to a 2014 University of Pennsylvania study, for example. Today's parents are under a great deal of pressure to provide family meals, which are associated with a decrease in childhood obesity, for their kids. But by and large the culture around food and eating has changed for the worse.

A

Nowhere are these changes more obvious than at work. More than 62 per cent of the American workforce eats lunch at their desks. In Ireland, more than 50 per cent do, while 39 per cent of Canadians eat their midday meal at their workstation. Often, this is not a wholesome bagged lunch prepared at home. It is fast food, convenience store food or frozen food.

In addition to the overeating that comes from distraction, eating at your workstation only exacerbates another dire health risk – sitting all day – and it also keeps you from experiencing the benefits of connecting with others over a shared meal.

Work, travel and isolation all put the body under stress, and stress and meals would ideally not mix. For one thing, you are much more likely to experience acid reflux when you eat while experiencing stress, especially if you are eating the type of unhealthy foods that cause heartburn. Even worse, the very chemicals your body churns out while stressed (namely cortisol and insulin) are the same ones that signal to your body to store calories as fat. It can also contribute to other sorts of digestive upsets, including constipation or diarrhoea.

Acid reflux is a common condition in which stomach acid backs up into the oesophagus, the tube that connects the throat to the stomach.

Heartburn is the more colloquial term for acid reflux.

Cortisol is a multi-functional hormone. It is commonly known as the stress hormone because it rises in tense situations. High levels of cortisol contribute to weight gain.

The COVID-19 global pandemic of 2020 has left people feeling more confined than ever. With people working from home, mealtimes become blurred and all-day snacking can replace a more traditional breakfast, lunch and dinner. A survey of European eating habits during March and April 2020 conducted by Statista revealed that 27 per cent of respondents from the UK reported that their eating habits had declined during the pandemic.

Food culture, like all aspects of culture, is created and upheld at a societal level. Farming systems, food production, global eating patterns and the environments we live and eat in cannot be refashioned overnight. Changing it will take a rethinking of shared values across families, communities, companies and countries.

A   Whether in an office in London, UK, or in a call centre in Cape Town, South Africa, eating lunch alone at your desk is increasingly common. Eating while stressed or distracted is bad for your health.

Population growth after 1960 put pressure on the farming system. There was anxiety that existing forms of agriculture would not be able to meet the demands of an exploding global population. It was in the context of this perceived emergency that industrial farming was able to take over the food supply. Scientists manipulated nature in many ways. The goal was to produce more food, faster and cheaper. This pursuit shaped the way both plants and animals were produced, and ultimately, it fundamentally changed the foods we eat. Yes, industrial agriculture did result in more meat and vegetables grown in less time for less money. But how much did it also affect nutritional content or flavour in our food?

A

A   Overcrowded feedlots like this one in Fort Worth, Texas, create unhealthy conditions for livestock.

B   This illustration shows how poultry farmers have learned to raise fatter chickens, faster. In 2005, a two-month old bird weighed almost five times as much as its 1957 equivalent.

Population growth refers to the increase in the number of human being livings on the planet year on year. The global population currently grows by around 1.1 per cent a year.

Broiler chickens are chickens that have been bred specifically for meat production. They are typically six to eight weeks old when slaughtered.

INCREASE IN CHICKEN SIZE SINCE 1957
Relative growth from 0 to 56 days

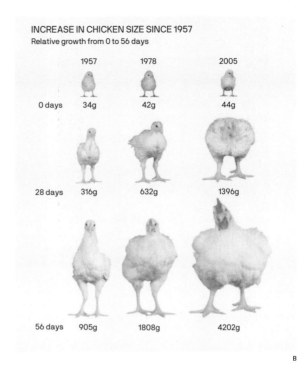

	1957	1978	2005
0 days	34g	42g	44g
28 days	316g	632g	1396g
56 days	905g	1808g	4202g

B

Let's look at the chicken as an example. In the 1940s chickens were expensive. They were also small. The broiler chickens of the day typically weighed only 700 grams (1½ lb). Today, supermarket chickens are usually 2.25 kilograms (5 lb) or more. But what they lacked in size, they made up for in flavour – a rich, savoury, deeply 'chicken-y' flavour. It is common to hear older people bemoan that chicken does not taste like it used to, and they are not wrong.

In the UK, amid the food shortages and rationing of World War II, many households began keeping chicken coups in their backyard to ensure inexpensive access to chicken and eggs. But in the United States, there was a different trend in poultry. In the mid-1940s, the US Department of Agriculture (USDA) held a contest to breed a bigger, better chicken. It was called the 'Chicken of Tomorrow' contest, and participants were encouraged to breed for size, specifically breast size. Flavour was not something these 'better' chickens were evaluated on.

A

B

A José Olé brand frozen chicken and cheese taquitos is an example of a highly processed food with close to 100 ingredients.

B A box of fried chicken balls from a convenience store, or *konbini*, in Tokyo, Japan, is another example of a highly processed food that contributes to obesity.

C Employees arrange frozen chicken fillets into bags at a food processing plant in Chok Chai, Nakhon Ratchasima province, Thailand.

From that point onwards, chickens became bigger and, notably, blander. The carbohydrate-rich diet chickens need to become fat fast does nothing to create flavour. On pre-industrial traditional farms, chickens would have spent time on pasture eating earthworms, insects and wild seeds. Now the animals are raised quickly and harvested while they are still very young, they never develop the richer, deeper flavour of more mature birds.

As chicken lost its inherent flavour, the processed food industry was figuring out how to add it back in. Today, a majority of chicken is not sold plain and fresh, it is injected and marinated, battered, breaded and fried. It is highly seasoned, salt-filled and found in the frozen food aisle or in fast food restaurants.

Almost every ingredient added by the processed food industry is a hazard to human health.

Shelf life is how long a food product kept in storage will stay fresh and safe to eat.

Precision fermentation technology enables the programming of microorganisms to produce complex organic molecules, such as proteins and vitamins, with precise specifications, including taste and colour.

All food produced by factory farms has been bred to maximize yield, speed, size and shelf life while minimizing expenditure. Natural flavour and nutrient content are, at best, a tangential concern. Tomatoes and strawberries are two more common foods whose flavour has been all but eradicated by Big Food. Champions of the developing precision fermentation technology argue that they will be able to retain the natural flavours and nutrients of all foods without adding ingredients that are harmful to human health.

c

Though flavour is not a priority for big agriculture, it is definitely a major concern of the packaged and prepared food industry. While the robust natural flavours of food have been muted by industrial agriculture, flavour scientists have worked out how to turn raw ingredients such as chicken, corn and soy into food products that have been formulated with just the right amount of sugar, salt and fat in just-right ratios to light up the same pleasure seeking parts of the brain that are stimulated by hard drugs like cocaine.

The result is that the majority of supermarket and restaurant foods is calorie-dense, nutrient-poor and very difficult to stop eating. Processed foods also tend to lack fibre, which is a key element of a healthy diet. Fibre-rich foods fill the stomach, sending signals to the brain that it is time to stop eating. Real food also usually needs to be chewed more than soft-textured ultra-processed food, and the act of chewing is also associated with better satiety – the feeling of fullness and satisfaction that makes you want to stop eating.

A

Fibre is the part of a plant that the body does not digest. There are two types: soluble and insoluble. Both keep your digestive system in good working order and are beneficial to health.

Bliss point is a term used by food scientists and manufacturers to describe optimally pleasurable levels of salt, sugar and fat in products.

A   Pringles are made not with whole potato slices, but a mixture of potato flakes, water, and cornstarch that is shaped into identical chips to perfectly fit in the can.
B   These photos show the actual amount of sugar found in common supermarket products. Manufacturers add high quantities of sugar and salt to their products to get their flavour profile as close as possible to the 'bliss point'.

B

What started as a way to add flavour to foods that had lost their flavour has morphed into something more sinister. Today, food manufacturers hire top scientists to formulate food products in which the blend of flavours and textures reach the so-called 'bliss point'. This is when the flavour profile has been dialled in to trigger cravings and make you want to eat more and more of the food. In 2004 bliss point expert Howard Moskowitz (b. 1944) was hired by Cadbury Schweppes to formulate a new variety of Dr Pepper. In his pursuit of the perfect product he produced 61 different possible formulas, which were then put through 3,904 consumer taste tests to find the recipe closest to the bliss point. The end product was the hugely successful Cherry Vanilla Dr Pepper.

Hitting this bliss point often means adding sugar to foods you would not think of as being sweetened, for example, salad dressing or tomato sauce. Many pre-made pasta sauces have the same sugar content as a serving of cookies. To counter the perceptible sweetness, salt content in these foods tends to rise as sugar does. It is no wonder that processed foods contribute to both type 2 diabetes and hypertension.

A

A People dressed as Domino's pizza, Taco Bell taco sauce and a Dairy Queen Blizzard. Corporate fast foods are relentlessly marketed to consumers.

B In these advertisements from the 1950s, the British Egg Marketing Board encourages people to enjoy a whole foods based breakfast, using a slogan by author Fay Weldon (b. 1931).

Many people living with excess weight or obesity blame themselves for a lack of willpower, an inability to resist the foods that surround them in an obesogenic environment. But there is nothing wrong with them – the foods themselves were engineered by a slew of scientists not simply to be tasty but to be downright addictive.

These foods affect our bodies and our brains in the short and long term. Imagine waking up on the day of a big work presentation and having the time to enjoy breakfast at home. You simmer a pot of wholegrain oats with raisins and shredded apple. While it cooks, you toast some walnuts, make coffee and slice a grapefruit. It is a meal that leaves you feeling full and satisfied but not heavy or sluggish. Best of all, thanks to fibre from the oats and protein and healthy fats from the nuts, you will be energized and full until lunch.

Now picture the alternative. Maybe you stayed up too late cramming for the presentation, but you have no time to make breakfast at home. Instead, you swing by the drive-through for a bagel with sausage, egg and cheese, plus a chocolate flavoured coffee drink topped with whipped cream. You eat it in your car.

In scenario A, you knock it out of the park with your presentation. Your mind feels sharp and your body is energized. Afterwards you bask in accolades from your team, you treat everyone to lunch from that expensive gourmet salad place. It is the most productive afternoon your department has had all quarter!

But what happens in scenario B? You arrive at work with a slight stomach ache, but somehow you are also still hungry. Maybe you are experiencing brain fog and you struggle to remember how you wanted to articulate all the points in your PowerPoint. You muddle through, and when it is over you are so hungry you eat two doughnuts. Now you have a headache and spend the afternoon scrolling Facebook.

B

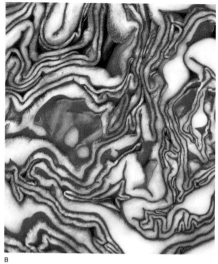

A

B

Most people have experienced some version
of both of these situations. We know that the
kind of food we use to fuel our bodies affects
how we perform, especially our brains. Though
it accounts for only 2 per cent of our body
weight, the brain consumes 20 per cent of
the calories we eat. And what you feed it
really affects how it does its job.

Junk food (highly processed or
fast food) is particularly detrimental
to brain function. In the short term,
foods that create unstable blood
sugar (low-fibre, refined carbohydrates, high fat foods) inhibit
our ability to do our best thinking.
But over the long term, the effects
of a Western style diet are even
more pronounced: a World Health
Organization report from 2019 found
that eating a healthy diet could
help reduce the risk of dementia.

C

D

A   Fresh blueberries are packed with vitamins and antioxidants.
B   Red cabbage is one of the healthiest vegetables you can eat. The WHO recommends people eat 250 grams (9 oz) of vegetables every day.
C   Thanks to its excellent nutrition profile, kale is considered by nutrition experts to be a superfood.
D   Salmon is one food few people eat enough of. The American Heart Association recommends two to three servings of fish weekly.

A study led by Felice Jacka in 2015 suggested that a Western style diet actually shrinks the brain. Specifically, it is associated with a smaller hippocampus. The hippocampus is an important area of the brain involved in regulating motivation, memory, learning and emotions. Other studies have suggested a link between a typical Western diet and depression. Those who eat more processed meat, fried foods, refined carbohydrates and sweet snacks show more signs of depression than peers who eat a diet rich in fruits and vegetables.

This is significant because depression can be as fatal as heart disease. The World Health Organization reports that there is one death from suicide every 40 seconds, and that between 2005 and 2015 the number of people suffering from depression worldwide increased by 18.4 per cent. Diet is certainly not the only contributing factor to depression, but it is a factor you can modify.

A

B

What you eat shapes your mood, and of course it shapes your body. But the relationship been food and weight is not as simple as it is often portrayed in the media and even by doctors. If you have ever wanted to lose a few pounds, you have probably been offered the following pat advice: eat less and move more. The proposition of weight loss is often boiled down to truisms like 'calories in, calories out'. These axioms oversimplify the intricate energy balancing act in the human body that largely determines what you weigh.

This way of thinking about body size makes it seem like losing weight is as simple as saying no to second helpings at dinner and perhaps taking the stairs instead of the elevator. It makes it sound like anyone with the average measure of human intelligence and the slightest self control can easily lose weight and keep it off. But of course, as the bleak statistics around long term weight loss can attest, there is clearly something missing from this picture. Many brilliant people with all the financial resources in the world struggle with their weight all their lives. Often, it costs them their lives.

Approaches to weight loss that hinge on counting calories do not discriminate between a candy bar and a head of broccoli. If you are on a calorie restricted diet, the assumption is that it does not matter what you eat as long as you stay within your allotted calorie budget.

You can have a Big Mac for dinner for 540 calories or you can have a cup of black beans, a cup of brown rice and a large pile of steamed kale drizzled with olive oil for about 500 calories. While the 'calories in, calories out' camp would suggest it does not matter which you choose, the truth is that these two meals set off a cascade of hormonal and biological response that will drive your eating behaviour during the rest of the day.

c

A   Celebrities like Kim Kardashian advertise for companies selling questionable weight loss products, such as appetite suppressant lollipops.

B   Social media influencer Kylie Jenner advertises a so-called 'detox' tea that claims, without scientific evidence, to promote fat burning and weight loss.

C   In recent years, laws have compelled restaurants to list calorie information on food menus, as seen at this McDonald's in Cambridgeshire, UK.

The fat, white flour and, yes, sugar (a Big Mac contains more than 2 teaspoons of sugar) contained in a burger is counteracted by only 3 grams (¹¹/₁₀₀ oz) of fibre. Black beans, brown rice and kale has eight times that amount – about 24 grams (⅘ oz) of fibre, and zero added sugar. The burger also contains 28 grams (1 oz) of fat (10 of them saturated fat). The similarity in calorie counts belies staggering nutritional differences in these two meals.

Within minutes of eating that burger, your blood sugar shoots up. Insulin is pumped out fast and furious by the pancreas. In the long term, this leads to insulin resistance and type 2 diabetes. In the short term it leads to a sluggish post-dinner period followed by a renewed appetite way before you should be hungry again, which likely results in late night snacking. High levels of ghrelin, known as the hunger hormone, is being produced in the gut and is signalling to the brain that you are hungry.

A

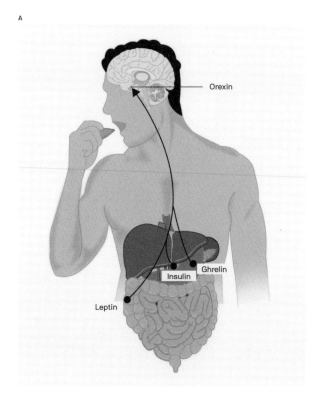

Orexin

Insulin

Ghrelin

Leptin

Whole foods are foods sold in their natural, unprocessed state. Examples include apples, leafy greens and fresh cuts of meat.

A   This illustration shows some of the hormones that work together to affect eating behaviour. Orexin influences sleep, arousal, appetite and energy expenditure; leptin inhibits hunger and regulates energy balances; insulin regulates glucose in the blood; and the 'hunger hormone' ghrelin increases appetite.

B   Fibre-rich beans and lentils help control blood sugar and maintain a healthy body weight.

B

When you eat the fibre-filled beans and rice, on the other hand, blood sugar remains steady. You have put a much larger volume of food in your stomach, literally filling you up and activating stretch receptors in your stomach that communicate to your brain that you are full, and you will have no blood sugar crash later on, prompting cravings for more junk food. This meal lets your brain's fullness hormone – leptin – do its job.

Think of the human body like a computer and our diet as a program. Feed yourself a steady stream of highly processed foods and the program will instruct your body to produce more hormones that drive hunger, cravings and weight gain, leading to obesity, diabetes and other diseases. But feed your body with nutrient-dense whole foods, low in refined sugar and carbohydrates and high in fibre, and the program will do what evolution has wired it to do, restoring the healthy hunger and fullness signals that contribute to a healthy, stable body weight. The modern industrial food system, with its surfeit of highly processed foods, and weight gain is inevitable.

A

A/B Production of gummy bear fruit gums in the Haribo candy factory in Bonn, west Germany. These popular sweets are sugar-laden and artificially flavoured.

Butylated hydroxytoluene (BHT) is an artificial chemical preservative found in many processed food items.

Bisphenol A (BPA) is a compound used in the lining of cans and boxes that contain food. It is toxic and can leach into the food.

Patrially hydrogenated describes oils that have had hydrogen injected into them so they stay solid at room temperature. They are used instead of natural fats to extend shelf life.

If you have ever glanced at a packaged food label, you know there is more to consider than the macronutrients – fat, protein and carbohydrates. In the era of Big Food, the packaged groceries that line supermarket shelves and pack the freezer section are full of ingredients most people never keep in their home kitchen or use in scratch cooking or baking. You will know these ingredients by their unfamiliar names. They have a high tech, scientific ring to them.

In his book *In Defence of Food* (2008) author Michael Pollan famously advised against eating anything your great-grandmother would not recognize as food. She probably would never have heard of butylated hydroxytoluene (BHT) or bisphenol A (BPA), for example. Though she may have cooked with corn syrup, it was certainly not high fructose corn syrup. Her fats were not, as many around the world are today, partially hydrogenated.

B

So what is the problem with this modern plethora of preservatives, additives and flavour enhancers? Despite Pollan's common sense advice, there is still a lot of controversy. For one thing, many of these ingredients lengthen shelf life, guard against harmful bacteria and prevent spoilage. In many ways, processing and the chemicals it brings into the food have saved lives by making it possible to store food safely for long periods of time and by cutting down on contaminated food and food-borne illnesses.

However, it is impossible to ignore the fact that its widespread use in the industrial food system corresponds closely with the rise of obesity.

A Pineapples, one of nature's sweetest fruits, are typically drenched in a sugar syrup during packaging.
B Workers guide sterilized hot cans of pineapple towards cold water ready for packaging at the Samroiyod Corp. fruit processing facility in Pranburi, Pranchuap Khiri Khan, Thailand.
C Rows of cans of Campbell's condensed tomato soup on the shelves of a grocery store. In 2016 Campbell's announced its plan to transition to using cans that do not contain BPA.

Bisphenol A (BPA) is a chemical often found in the lining of packaged food containers, such as canned tomatoes, and in plastics used for food storage. It prevents the food from taking on the flavour of the package. But studies have shown that the chemical does not simply stay on the can lining – it leaches into the food and people end up eating it.

This is a problem, because consuming BPA has been linked to many health problems including increased blood pressure and infertility. It is what is known as an endocrine disruptor; it interferes with the body's intricate system of hormones. It is legal in many countries, including the UK and USA, where the US Food and Drug Administration insists that the low levels in food are safe.

Partially hydrogenated oils, or 'trans fats', were ubiquitous in packaged foods, especially snacks and sweets, for years after their detrimental effects on heart health were proven. Denmark was the first country to heavily restrict industrially produced trans fats in food in 2003; it was followed by Austria, Switzerland, Iceland, Sweden and eventually the USA in 2018. Unfortunately, they remain common in lower- and middle-income countries, such as India and Brazil.

Manufacturers love these fats because they improve shelf life and save money. Trans fats are just about the worst kind for your heart. Even more so than saturated fats, they increase the bad kind of cholesterol (LDL) and decrease the good kind (HDL).

c

A   B

Butylated hydroxytoluene (BHT) and butylated hydroxyanisole (BHA) both play a role in preventing the fats in processed foods from becoming rancid. Many countries, including Australia, Canada, New Zealand, Japan and throughout Europe, have banned them because animal research strongly suggests they are likely to contribute to the development of cancer in humans. Other research indicates they could be toxic to cells. Other countries, including the USA, have no such ban, stating that these ingredients are 'generally recognized as safe'. It is up to harried consumers, too busy to read the fine print on packaging labels, to decide if the cookies or crisps are worth the possible risks.

Reading your ingredients list – not just the marketing language on a package – is the first step to making informed food choices. Or, as Michael Pollan would suggest, perhaps the best defence is choosing the type of whole foods that would have been recognized as food by your ancestors. These usually come without packaging or a label.

Unlabelled, non-packaged food is better from a nutritional perspective but it is also free from one of the most harmful things in our food supply:

Marketing. Most people dislike marketing and advertisements.

Moreover, most people believe ads have no effect on their own thinking or behaviour. Consciously, they register the irritation of a commercial interrupting their TV shows, Instagram feed or YouTube videos, but they give it little further thought.

Butylated hydroxyanisole (BHA) is a chemical additive that stabilizes the fats in processed foods.

A   This is the controversial preservative butylated hydroxytoluene, or BHT.
B   This is butylated hydroxyanisole, or BHA, a food additive used to increase shelf life in packaged foods.
C   Delivery services, such as the widely advertised Uber Eats, make it more convenient than ever to eat cheap and heavily processed fast food.
D   An advertisement for another delivery service, Deliveroo, on a public telephone phone box in Cork, Ireland.

C

D

The **prefrontal cortex** is the area of the brain responsible for complicated cognitive functioning, such as moderation and decision making.

When it comes to marketing, the average person does not understand themselves very well. In the United States alone, companies spend upward of $163 billion on advertising each year and the average American takes in more than 10,000 advertisements each day. This is a strategy that works: an overwhelming 90 per cent of consumers have been influenced by marketing to make some kind of purchasing decision. The way advertising affects you is below your conscious awareness.

This is especially true when it comes to food marketing. When we view the images typical of fast food restaurants – burger patties with appetizing grill marks, cheese melting just so, a pile of golden fries – it activates the pleasure centres of the brain, prompting craving at a biological level for the type of rich, calorie-packed food in the advertisement. Even if the ad was fleeting – a billboard you drove by, a Facebook post you hardly registered, product placement in a TV show you were not exactly focused on – it triggers craving in your brain in spite of the fact you do not realize what is happening.

A

McDonald's
Big Mac

Advertisement   Actual

Taco Bell
Crunchy Taco

Advertisement   Actual

Burger King
Whopper

Advertisement   Actual

McDonald's
Angus Deluxe Third Pounder

Advertisement   Actual

B

This effect is even more pronounced in children and teenagers, whose prefrontal cortexes are not fully developed. Meanwhile, a huge segment of all food marketing is aimed directly at children, priming them to eat all the processed and fast foods the adults in their lives will allow and contributing to weight gain and obesity.

Some parts of the world have policies in place to try to protect kids from the effects of food marketing. In the UK for example, there are standards about what advertising is acceptable during children's programming. Research shows that kids can recognize food brand logos by the age of two, demonstrating how powerful ads can be and making a case for such common sense regulations.

Yet many countries do nothing to protect children from food marketing. In fact, in the United States, about 50 per cent of all ads directed at kids are for food products. Fast food restaurants, soda and cereal are some of the most commonly advertised items. According to a 2012 report from the Federal Trade Commission, less than 0.5 per cent of food business's marketing budgets are spent promoting healthier items such as fruits and vegetables.

A

B

Polyculture is a type of farming that involves producing a mix of different crops and kinds of livestock, and promotes healthy soil.

Crop rotation is the practice of growing a certain series of different crops on the same piece of land from one growing season to the next.

Cover crops are planted in fields to replenish nutrients taken from the soil by crops that were previously grown there. Examples include oats, legumes and barley.

Another serious consequence of the proliferation of processed foods is the devastating impact it has had on the environment. The few crops used to make most processed food are crowding out everything else and diminishing biodiversity around the world with dire results.

It is estimated that there are more than 20,000 types of edible plants growing on the planet today, yet fewer than 20 of them represent 90 per cent of the crops people eat. In fact, only three plants (corn, wheat and rice) provide 60 per cent of the calories consumed around the world, according to the Food and Agriculture Organization of the United States. By some counts, more than three-quarters of the earth's biodiversity has already been lost.

This matters for many reasons. Eating a broad array of different foods helps ensure that people get a protective range of nutrients. Biodiversity also helps safeguard the food supply. If you grow many different varieties of a fruit and a disease or fungus occurs that wipes out one varietal, another can step in.

For instance, before the 1960s, most bananas were the Gros Michel banana, which was wiped out by a fungus. Today, 99 per cent of bananas grown for export are the Cavendish – chosen for its immunity to the fungus that wiped out the Gros Michel, and its ability to survive global travel. However, we now have no backup varieties of banana.

Before industrial agriculture, traditional farmers cultivated many different kinds of crops and animals, a technique referred to as a polyculture. Age-old methods, such as crop rotation, maintained soil health and promoted better crop yields naturally. Traditional farming also requires growing cover crops, which are coincidentally highly nutritious. Cover crops prevent erosion, control pests, bolster soil quality, sequester carbon and improve yields. But on a modern factory farm, where these jobs have been ignored or outsourced to chemicals, there is no incentive to grow these less profitable and largely unsubsidized foods.

C

D
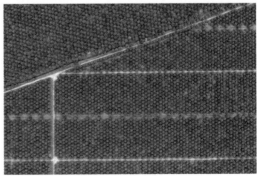

A   A man works on a banana farm in Carepa, Colombia. In 2019, a fungus that causes a disease in bananas that eventually stops them bearing fruit arrived in Latin America.
B   In an effort to prevent the spread of the crop-killing fruit fungus, an employee washes containers that will be used to export bananas.
C   An aerial view of land ploughed for sugar cane production near São Paulo, Brazil.
D   Palm oil trees growing in Perak, Malaysia. Palm oil is used in many processed foods. Its cultivation is a major driver of deforestation.

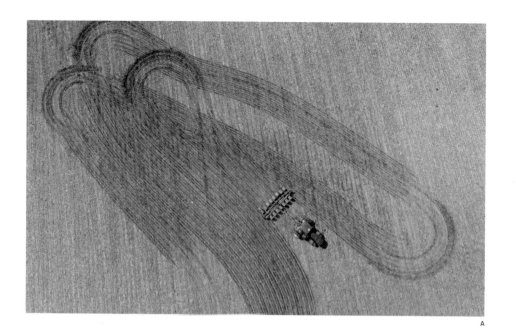

A

Today's large industrial farms do things differently. Typically monocultures, these farms usually produce a single food – milk, corn, pork, soybeans, wheat – across enormous swathes of land. Monoculture farming on this scale may have helped more people live with greater food security, but it wreaks havoc on the animals, workers and the environment in many ways.

Large-scale farming operations focus on the starchy, calorie-rich plants that provide reliable bumper crops and a dependable source of calories to feed an increasingly populated world. By growing just one or two varieties of a crop, the machinery and other processes used in production can be more standardized and therefore cheaper: a processing line built to move large, heavy Russet potatoes may not be able to deal with slender fingerling potatoes.

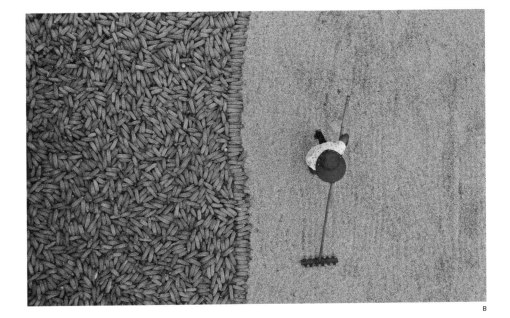

B

Monoculture means producing a single crop, such as corn, and is the standard practice of an industrial farm.

Food security is the condition of having the resources to ensure a household always has adequate nutrition.

One specific crop has proven especially problematic in terms of human health: corn.

As plants were bred for qualities prized by the global economy, including sweetness, the plants' characteristics have changed. Pre-industrial corn was roughly 2 per cent sugar. Today's corn has been bred over generations to be 'super sweet', and it contains about 20 times as much sugar. It also contains less protein, fibre and vitamins. Corn is grown in staggering quantities all around the world. More than 500 million tonnes of corn is produced annually by the two leading countries in corn production, the United States and China.

A   A soybean field in Illinois, USA. Soy in many forms is a staple ingredient in many processed foods found in the supermarket.

B   An aerial view of a villager drying corn in Chongqing, China.

THE HEALTH HAZARDS OF PROCESSED FOOD

73

Surprisingly little of that bounty is served up in a form anyone would recognize as the vegetable. Corn is an extremely versatile crop. It can be made into biofuel to power cars. Ground into flour, it becomes tortillas and chips. Certain types of corn are grown specifically to feed livestock on other factory farms. And a lot of it is turned into the high fructose corn syrup used to make junk food shelf stable for years.

So why is it that we have so very much corn when its impact on global health has been an increase in obesity and disease burden? The answer is because it is easy to grow on a large scale, making it ideal for feeding a growing world population cheaply while still allowing the Big Food business to make a profit.

Farming has always been an unpredictable business. So much depends on factors outside a farmer's control. Just think of how much the weather impacts how much can be grown in a year. Some growing seasons will be great and supply abundant, while others will be poor with most farmers having little or nothing to sell. This is one reason corn is so widely grown – once dried, it is sturdy on its own and it can also be turned into foodstuffs that are not especially perishable, such as high fructose corn syrup.

A

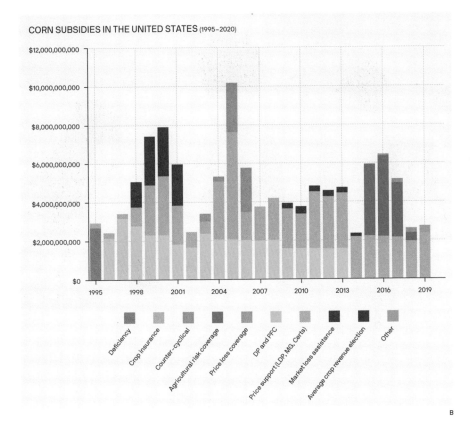

CORN SUBSIDIES IN THE UNITED STATES (1995–2020)

Legend: Deficiency, Crop insurance, Counter-cyclical, Agricultural risk coverage, Price loss coverage, DP and PFC, Price support (LDP, MG, Certs), Market loss assistance, Average crop revenue election, Other

B

Subsidies are monies supplied by governments to businesses, institutions or industries, either in the form of tax reductions or cash payments.

A   Many common household foods, including classic white Wonder Bread, Kraft Macaroni & Cheese and Heinz Tomato Ketchup, include corn as one of their ingredients.

B   A graph showing corn subsidies in the United States, and the various programmes that these payments were made through. These monies totalled $116.6 billion from 1995 to 2020.

These ups and downs in productivity are also why farm **subsidies** exist in almost every industrial country that farms. In the early days of these policies, when family farms were the norm rather than the exception, these subsidies kept payment stable, allowing a family farm to produce food in boom times when prices were low and in lean times when crops failed. Today, these benefits mostly accrue to large agribusiness. The EU pays out €65 billion per year in farm subsidies, and the United States is on track to spend $972.9 billion dollars on subsidies between 2014 and 2024.

A

Soda taxes impose an additional fee on sugar-sweetened beverages in order to discourage consumption and fund community programmes, often public health programmes.

But not all crops are subsidized. The commodities most heavily subsidized in the United States are corn, sugar, soybeans, wheat and livestock. These are not what most dietitians would call the building blocks of the kind of vegetable-heavy, whole-foods-based eating plan associated with positive health outcomes.

In many places, governments have tried to balance the scales somewhat with initiatives such as a soda tax. The thinking is that a higher price point will be a disincentive to purchasing soda, leading to decreased sugar consumption. And there are some indications it can work. In Mexico, where a soda tax was introduced in 2014, sales of sweetened drinks have come down by almost 10 per cent. Other countries that have introduced this type of tax include the UK, Ireland, Portugal, France and South Africa.

A   Health advocates at a rally in support of a proposed sugar tax in San Francisco, California, in 2014. A sugar tax was eventually introduced in San Francisco in 2016, though the soda industry spent nearly $20 million dollars attempting to defeat the initiative.

B   Primary school children eating their school lunch during the COVID-19 pandemic in Bangkok, Thailand. A nutritious meal provided at school is particularly important for economically disadvantaged children, who may not have easy access to healthy food at home. School closures during the COVID-19 pandemic have highlighted this issue.

Food policy affects what people eat.

As much as some want to frame food choices as an individual responsibility, governments play a huge role in creating an obesogenic or healthy food environment. Beyond the subsidies that shape the food supply itself and the taxes meant to influence consumer behaviour, there are myriad ways food policy can contribute to a population's overall health or risk of disease.

Policies determine what is on the menu in school lunch programmes as well as which categories of groceries people who receive public assistance can buy. Regulations can impact what kind of food marketing is allowed, when and where it can appear, and which populations it can target.

B

A

B

The industrial food system and factory farming have had a catastrophic effect on public health, the workers exploited by the system and on our environment. But even if you personally have largely opted out of the broken food system by growing your own food, shopping at your local farmers' market, avoiding restaurants and fast food outlets, and passing over processed products in favour of making meals from scratch, you still live in an ecosystem that is under assault and a climate that is becoming increasingly chaotic thanks in large part to industrial agriculture. There are no healthy people on a planet that can no longer support life.

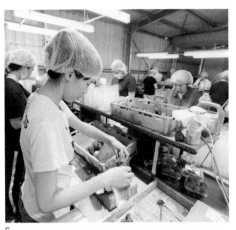
C

D

A   Kashmiri farmers harvest fresh strawberries near Srinagar, India. Around the world, strawberries are bred to maximize shelf life.

B   Monoculture growing operations like this strawberry farm in southwest France helps feed the constantly growing appetite for on-demand produce.

C   Strawberries are sorted and packed for market on the premises after being picked at this farm in Queensland, Australia.

D   A single Japan-grown strawberry, ensconced in styrofoam, paper, cardboard and plastic, is sold as a Valentine's day gift in Hong Kong. The strawberry sells for 168 Hong Kong dollars ($21.70).

Let's start by looking at a fairly recent phenomenon. All over the world, people enter supermarkets expecting a staggering variety of produce: peaches in the dead of winter; pineapples in Sweden; strawberries everywhere on the planet, 12 months of the year. In many of the places that strawberries grow naturally, they have a fleeting season of just a few weeks. But at some point, with the rise in transporting fruits and vegetables everywhere around the world, strawberries became a staple supermarket ingredient and now shoppers expect to find them every time they visit.

This demand for fresh produce all year round has fuelled the industrial farming practices that have led to tasteless berries and barren soil. And the transportation of food around the globe extracts its own cost on the planet. Planes and lorries require enormous amounts of the polluting fossil fuels that have contributed to a rapidly warming planet, fires that have decimated landscapes from California to Australia, and unstable weather patterns and events that bring dangerous storms, death and destruction. It has become clear that movement of foodstuffs around the globe on this scale is simply unsustainable.

One way to quantify this burden is in 'food miles'. The phrase refers to the distance food travels from its origin to the end consumer. Tim Lang, now a professor of Food Policy at City University, London, coined the term in the 1990s, and it remains an important part of the conversation about food and its environmental impact today. The 'food miles' racked up by all the stuff in your refrigerator contribute significantly to your carbon footprint. The situation has become so out of hand that it is common for fish caught in the United States to be shipped to China for processing and packing – before returning to the US.

It can be difficult to calculate food miles for any given food, but there are ways to estimate it, which can help make more informed shopping decisions. FoodMiles.com is one such online calculator. According to FoodMiles.com, Mexican avocados enjoyed in the United States represent 1,886 miles (3,034 km) travelled. But the environmental impact of any particular food goes deeper than the distance it travels. How it travels from one place to another is relevant. It is estimated that food that is flown uses 40 times more fuel than food that arrives via cargo ship.

A

Food miles are the distance a food item has travelled from where it was produced to where it is consumed.

A **carbon footprint** is the total amount of carbon emissions from the use of fossil fuels resulting from a specific person, event or group.

Farmers' markets are places local farmers gather to sell their crops to customers in their community.

B

C

Today, there is an international local food movement that advocates for communities defending their own local food shed as a way to reduce the harms of extravagant food miles and shore up local economies. This may involve shopping at farmers' markets and eating in season. It means going without strawberries in the winter. Some people, known as locavores, take these values to the extreme and commit to eating only what is grown within 100 miles (161 km) of their home.

A   Labelling goods with their carbon footprint can help people make decisions about how to spend their food budget.

B   Farmers who sell directly to consumers can grow peach varieties that taste great and concern themselves less with shelf life.

C   Buying directly from local growers such as Spring Dell Farm in Littleton, Massachusetts, USA, helps keep money in the local economy.

The values of the local food movement go beyond environmental motivations. Local food, grown on smaller, old fashioned farms, tends to be more flavourful and more nutritious as well, because it can be bred to prize those characteristics. Producers who ship their products half way around the world via planes, trains, trucks and boats tend to breed for durability over all else, so their goods can survive the rigors of travel and still look appealing on the grocery store shelf. So it is well worth while making this alternative local food system more accessible to more people.

A

B

Imported produce is only one aspect of modern agribusiness that is hastening global warming and creating climate change. In fact, the majority of environmental harm from our current food system happens during production. Since the 1950s, worldwide grain production has quadrupled. As the population grew and workers moved away from rural farming communities into city environments, it became urgent to produce a lot more food to feed the urbanizing world.

How did farmers do it? Part of the answer lies in chemistry, specifically inorganic fertilizers.

One of the main nutrients all plants need to grow is nitrogen, and plenty of it. Traditional poly-culture farms enriched the soil with nitrogen in earth-friendly, low-tech ways. Though they did not have the formal scientific knowledge to understand the mechanism behind it, early 20th-century farmers did know that if they applied compost and plant and animal waste to the soil, the crops that they grew would be healthier and their yields more robust.

A Carbon emissions from trucking are just one part of the overall carbon footprint of our food supply chain.

B A Costco warehouse stacked with produce including asparagus, strawberries, pineapples and clementines. Produce from every corner of the globe, all year round, has become a baseline expectation for shoppers.

C Fertilizing soil with manure, as is being done by this horse-drawn manure spreader in Iowa, USA, in 1941, is a practice centuries old.

D Manure spreaders and other more natural means of adding nitrogen to the soil via plant and animal waste kept the environmental impacts of farming much lower than modern methods do.

A

Those farmers understood crop rotation and cover crops, farming practices that naturally recharge the soil with nitrogen after it has been depleted from harvesting other crops. As scientists grew to understand the all-important role of nitrogen in plant growth, the well-intentioned but ultimately disastrous quest for a synthetic nitrogen fertilizer began.

During World War II, nitrogen made from fossil fuels was used to manufacture munitions. Nitrogen is explosive and even today, fertilizer factories and the lorries that move it are vulnerable to deadly explosions. After the war, those factories pivoted to making more and more nitrogen-based fertilizer for agriculture. Agribusiness decided dousing the food supply with an explosive and environmentally damaging chemical was the ticket to bigger and bigger profits.

Any use of fossil fuels is bad news for the environment. Every aspect of using them, from extracting them, to transporting them to burning them for fuel, throws toxic compounds into the air that drive global warming and compromise human health. Inorganic fertilizers also commonly contain phosphorus, potassium and sulphur. Today, chemical fertilizers are often made from natural gas, which is obtained increasingly through what is commonly known as fracking.

Fracking is a relatively new technology and the effects of the practice are not fully understood. Earthquakes have occurred near some fracking sites around the world, and studies, such as those by Michael Brudzinski in the USA in 2019 and the British Geological Survey in the UK in 2011, suggest that it is probable that the fracking caused these seismic events.

Fracking involves drilling into shale rock and then injecting a mixture of chemicals, water and sand to extract natural gas trapped in the shale rock for use as fuel.

It is estimated that the annual use of chemical fertilizers is more than 200 million tonnes globally, and in spite of how clearly harmful it is, the practice continues to grow. The consequences of this are cascading.

B

All this nitrogen is sprayed onto farmland, and much of it runs off into the surrounding water table. This sets off a whole new chain of environmental disasters. As nitrogen flows into the world's rivers and oceans, it continues to act as a fertilizer, feeding algae and reducing the oxygen levels in the water. It creates dead zones, wide swathes of ocean where oxygen concentrations are so low it kills of the vast majority of marine wildlife in the area. This reduces biodiversity further. Nitrogen in the ocean is also speeding the destruction of coral reefs, where algae blooms obstruct sunlight.

Decades of applying chemical fertilizers degrades the soil in still other ways. The nutrients in soil do not just help plants grow, they help hold the soil together. Soil that has been artificially fertilized becomes less and less robust over time, becoming more vulnerable to erosion. A rich soil maintained by a knowledgeable farmer with organic fertilizers, such as compost and manure, and crop rotation, does not wash away easily when it rains. In fact, healthy soil actually absorbs water like a sponge and requires less irrigation (another environmentally problematic practice).

A

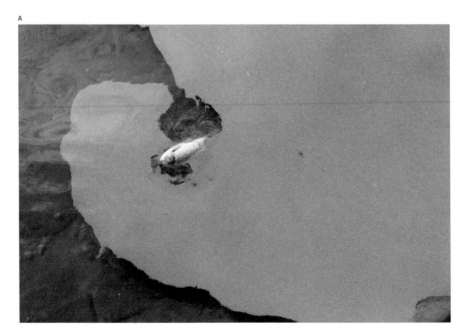

Compost is decaying organic matter intended to be used as a fertilizer for plants.

Manure is animal waste. It releases nitrogen into the soil slowly, encouraging plant growth and avoiding plant 'burn' that can occur with synthetic nitrogen.

Irrigation is a system for watering crops at regular intervals.

Herbicides kill unwanted plants that compete with a farmer's stalks of corn and fields of wheat. They can be natural or artificial.

B

C

Inorganic chemical-based fertilizers are not the only suspect substance sprayed on farmland and the crops that eventually become our food. There is an array of chemicals meant to do jobs that once were done by skilled farmers and Mother Nature. Herbicides, used for eradicating any weeds competing with crops, and pesticides, used to kill plant, fungal or animal pests, are among the most concerning. These substances may also be destroying our health.

A   Nitrogen continues to act as fertilizer after it enters our rivers, causing algae blooms, like this one in China, that can be harmful to wildlife and humans.

B   Chemical herbicides such as RoundUp, like inorganic fertilizers, have largely displaced older, less environmentally damaging methods.

C   RoundUp has been repeatedly called out by those protesting against the dangers of genetically modified organisms (GMOs).

From the late 1970s to 2016, there was a 100-fold increase in the application of herbicides worldwide. What's the harm of a little weed killer in the salad bar? The most widely used herbicide worldwide is glyphosate. In 2015, the World Health Organization's International Agency for Research on Cancer classed glyphosate as a probable carcinogen. In 2017 the European Chemicals Agency found that it caused eye damage and was toxic to aquatic ecosystems, but it stopped short of labelling it a carcinogen.

A Targeted applications of pesticides are used to control locust swarms like this one in northern Kenya in 2020, part of the worst locust outbreak in decades.
B An Egyptian farmer sprays a wheat field with pesticides in the northern Nile delta, Egypt.
C Protesters in Rome, Italy, demand a ban on neonicotinoid insecticides, which are harmful to the bees and other pollinators that our farmed food depends on.

Pesticides control insects, rodents, mould and fungus. Though there are known health hazards from pesticides at high doses, current science holds that the average amount of pesticide residue found in the food we eat is safe. This judgement is controversial, and, as with herbicides, many people seek to avoid them, citing the long list of substances once considered safe that were later banned.

In the United States, the Environmental Working Group releases a *Shopper's Guide* annually to help inform consumers about which specific fruits and vegetables are most and least contaminated. The 2019 guide shows that USDA tests revealed kale to be one vegetable that is particularly contaminated. The *Shopper's Guide* states that 92 per cent of kale samples contained pesticide residues. Dacthal (DCPA) was the most common pesticide found on kale. The Environmental Protection Agency labelled it a possible carcinogen in 1995; it has been banned in Europe since 2005.

ADHD is an acronym for attention deficit hyperactivity disorder. It may cause difficulty concentrating and controlling impulses.

Herbicides and pesticides are relatively new, making it impossible to know the long term health consequences they may turn out to have. Often, chemicals that were previously considered safe are later banned because new research overturns that older 'generally recognized as safe' conclusion. Whether these substances will eventually be found to contribute to cancer, ADHD or other conditions is an open question. In the meantime, many people choose organic produce at the super-market without realizing that there are many organic-approved 'natural' pesticides that may have health consequences of their own.

The sweeping changes in agriculture allowed another unforeseen threat to emerge: superbugs. These are pathogenic bacteria that are increasingly resistant to the drugs that used to treat them effectively.

The original antibiotic was penicillin. Discovered in the late 1920s and put into widespread use in the 1940s, penicillin was a life saving miracle medicine. Before we had antibiotics, even minor infections from cuts could cause death. Any type of bacterial infection was a very serious problem. Today, common ailments like urinary tract infections are nothing more than an annoyance; a single course of antibiotics cures it quickly.

c

Since their discovery, over use of these wonder drugs has led to bacteria evolving and developing resistance to antibiotics. Increasingly, the bacteria that cause infections do not respond to the same treatment that would have been effective five or ten years before. Bacteria such as *Clostridium difficile* are called 'superbugs' because antibiotics cannot knock them out.

According to the Centers for Disease Control and Prevention (CDC) in the United States, 14,000 deaths annually can be chalked up to *C. difficile* spreading unchecked thanks to antibiotic resistance. CDC data indicates that antibiotic resistance claims 25,000 lives in the United States each year. In the European Union, it results in 23,000 deaths annually. By 2050, some experts forecast 10 million deaths annually, which would make it the leading cause of death on the planet. The industrial food system has helped create this crisis, and the fact that they are not held accountable in any way for reversing this trend is outrageous.

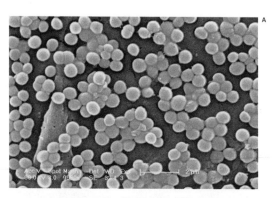
A

Antibiotic resistance results from the overuse of antibiotic drugs. Bacteria evolve a resistance to the drug, creating so-called 'superbugs' that cannot be effectively treated.

B

A   Methicillin-resistant *Staphylococcus aureus* (MRSA), seen here through an electron microscope, can cause dangerous infections that resist most treatments.
B   The *Staphylococcus aureus* bacterium is commonly found on our skin and is normally harmless, but can cause serious infections if it breaks through the skin barrier.
C   Antibiotics are used in vast quantities in cattle feedlots like this one, to keep cows healthy in overcrowded pens.

c

The consequences of antibiotic resistance are already dire and potentially catastrophic. But its primary driver remains largely hidden. When most people think about antibiotic over use, they think of doctors writing prescriptions for colds and other viruses that do not respond to antibiotics. That is part of the problem, but it is nothing compared to the over use of anti-biotics that happens in concentrated animal feeding operations (CAFOs).

Livestock are dosed with antibiotics for two reasons: to treat infection and to boost growth. Just as with humans, antibiotics are used to treat bacterial infections after they have been discovered in animals. The crowded, cruel and filthy conditions in CAFOs are breeding grounds for infections: animals are usually kept in extremely close quarters; their excrement flows freely and sanitation practices are lax. As a result, there is a lot of animal sickness in a feedlot. Livestock are therefore often given antibiotics prophylactically as well.

A

A   Greenpeace activists campaign against the excessive use of antibiotics in livestock farming in front of discount food retailer Lidl in Berlin, Germany.
B   With antibiotic-resistant bacteria on the rise, it has become more important than ever for hospitals like this one in England to take precautions against possibly deadly infections.
C   Tomatoes are washed in bleach at a processing plant in Florida, USA, to prevent contamination from salmonella and other pathogens common in industrial farming.

B

In addition to treating disease, antibiotics promote weight gain. In recent years, this practice has been banned in several countries, making it legal to administer antibiotics to livestock for therapeutic reasons only. The World Health Organization has also come out strongly against the practice. Sadly, current laws do not go far enough to meaningfully address enough of industrial agriculture's harmful practices.

As of 2017, any antibiotic important for human health cannot legally be used to fatten up livestock in the United States. In the European Union, the practice has been banned since 2006. In many less wealthy nations around the world, it is still common to give livestock antibiotics routinely as part of the animal feed, continuing to fuel the rise of antibiotic resistance. Bacteria has no national identity; it is a global problem that requires a co-operative global solution. A great deal of damage has already been done, rendering many of the most powerful drugs less effective than they once were. For example, the superbug methicillin-resistant *Staphylococcus aureus* (MRSA), does not respond to antibiotics at all.

Another threat common on the factory farm is the bacterium salmonella. It causes food-borne illness in the form of stomach upset, vomiting and diarrhoea. In the United States, it causes more than 1 million illnesses each year, and 19,000 of those people end up in the hospital. Hundreds of people die.

Salmonella is found in many everyday foods. Though it originates in the digestive tract in animals, it has been found in all kinds of non-animal foods, including vegetables and peanut butter. So how do bacteria from the digestive tract in an animal or person get into your peanut butter? In one case, a leaky roof at a peanut butter factory was suspected. The water likely mixed with bird faeces before it dripped over the production line.

But the vast majority of salmonella outbreaks start as a result of industrial factory farm practices. Water runoff from a CAFO where cattle are raised can carry salmonella downstream to farms growing lettuce, another way in which this animal-based pathogen finds its way into vegetable-based foods.

c

A Protesters dressed as chlorinated chickens during a demonstration against President Trump's visit to the UK in 2019. It is feared by some that a post-Brexit trade deal between the UK and US would mean chlorine-washed chicken – currently banned in the EU – would be imported to the UK.
B Eggs rolling down a conveyor belt at this farm in Maine, USA, are under extra scrutiny after salmonella contamination at a related farm led to the recall of 380 million eggs.
C Hundreds of hens packed into crowded hen houses like this one increase the likelihood of bacterial contamination in their eggs.

Beef, especially ground beef, has been frequently recalled in the United States due to salmonella contamination, and in 2020 a British dog food manufacturer had to recall its products due to the possible presence of salmonella in the beef. During the butchering process, if a knife slips and the digestive tract of a steer is punctured, faecal matter can easily contaminate the surrounding meat. When parts of that animal are then ground for ground beef, and that beef is mixed with the beef from hundreds or even thousands of other animals, that is a recipe for a widespread, multi-location salmonella outbreak.

Chicken flesh is also a common carrier of salmonella. Over the years, testing has shown that much of the raw chicken supply is contaminated with the bacteria. This is why there is such an emphasis on fully cooking chicken in all forms to 75°C (167°F) – heat kills the bacteria.

A

Chlorine is a chemical used to make a solution commonly used to wash chickens with the intention of killing bacteria to prevent food-borne illness.

B

Free range is a term used to suggest that livestock were allowed to roam freely outdoors and graze on pasture.

c

In the United States, it is common for processors to wash chickens with a chlorine solution in an effort to kill salmonella and other bacteria. In Europe, this practice has been banned since 1997. Though people think the chlorine itself poses a threat, it does not. The problem is that plants that chlorinate their chicken tend to have more lax sanitation because of it. Worse, a 2018 study from Southampton University found that salmonella and other disease-causing bacteria remain active even after a chlorine wash. The chlorine washing process does however render the bacteria undetectable in a lab, creating a false sense of security.

Eggs, even free range ones, may also be contaminated, either on the outside, due to improper handling or sanitation, or inside their shell, which is why you see warnings on restaurant menus about the risks of eating undercooked eggs. While few diners prefer their chicken breast medium rare, many people like their yolks runny, a cooking technique that does not sufficiently heat the egg to kill the bacteria. Large scale egg-producing operations tightly packed with egg-laying hens, can be shockingly unsanitary, with more than enough manure in evidence to increase the risk of those eggs becoming contaminated.

E. coli is a rod-shaped bacterium that lives in the digestive system of both people and animals. Most strains are harmless, but some cause severe and sometimes fatal illness.

Like salmonella, E. coli is yet another intractable problem of the industrial food system for both meat products and vegetables. In 2018, just before the United States' biggest food holiday, Thanksgiving, home cooks were told to throw away any romaine lettuce they might have in the refrigerator. The recall was unusually large, covering not specific stores or brands but all romaine, everywhere. In addition, consumers were asked to sanitize their produce drawers and anything else the lettuce may have touched.

It was the most sweeping of many recent romaine lettuce recalls. Unbelievably, the greens have been contaminated with E. coli repeatedly. In 2019, again just before Thanksgiving, it happened once more. In fact, romaine has been recalled four times in less than three years in the United States. In spite of the most recent recall, at least 167 people were infected and 85 were hospitalized; and 15 people developed kidney failure. Everyone survived the 2019 outbreak. Since 2017, in the United States and Canada combined, seven people have died from contaminated romaine.

B

The reason these recalls are so broad, affecting dozens of states when they happen, is that almost all of the romaine consumed in the United States and Canada comes from two locations: California's Salinas Valley and Yuma, Arizona. The lettuce is grown over many thousands of acres, adjacent to other types of factory farming operations. The popularity of romaine lettuce means that the scale is industrial, and this is very likely part of the problem. Foods grown on a smaller, more human scale are very often safer and healthier.

Another contributing factor is that romaine, and most other lettuces for that matter, grow on the ground. Unlike other types of crops that may be elevated on trees or vines, or foods that have a protective skin you peel away before eating, romaine is very vulnerable to contaminants in the soil as well as any bacteria that may be mixed in to the water used to irrigate these enormous fields. And of course, unlike potatoes and crops that grow on the ground, romaine is nearly always eaten raw. The protective step of cooking, which heats bacteria enough to kill it, is removed.

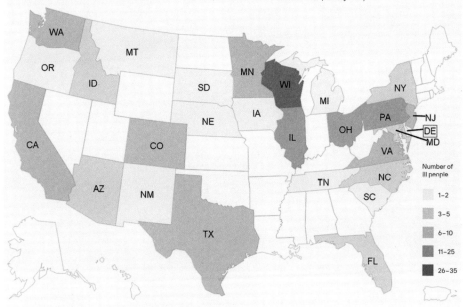

Number of ill people

- 1–2
- 3–5
- 6–10
- 11–25
- 26–35

A

A A map of the US showing the number of E. coli cases per state caused by an outbreak in January 2020. States are coloured according to the number living there who became ill.

B Labour conditions at meat packing plants also lead to disease outbreaks among workers, such as the COVID-19 outbreak at this German plant in 2020.

Experts such as Amanda J. Deering believe that romaine is not more susceptible to this E. coli contamination than other vegetables grown in similar settings – in 2006 an E. coli outbreak was linked to spinach – it is only that romaine is vastly more popular. It has long been the first choice of consumers as well as food service for salads and anything served on a bed of greens: there is a lot more romaine growing in California than kale. So those who have eschewed romaine in favour of spring mix or butter lettuce are not necessarily safe from this kind of food-borne illness, unfortunately.

These types of massive recalls are less common in other parts of the world with better oversight and regulations. The United States is 21 out 125 countries that Oxfam America ranked for a healthy food supply in 2014, below most wealthy nations. The FDA reports that it continues to evaluate the problem. Clearly the efforts are not enough.

It is not just the end consumer who faces the hazards of industrial food production. The workers at meat packing plants and on large scale farms have some of the most dangerous jobs on the planet – and that was before COVID-19 hit. Factory farm workers, whether they are outside in fields or inside meat packing plants, are vulnerable to repetitive stress injuries as well as accidents with the dangerous equipment they work with. They are exposed to chemicals, such as pesticides, in higher concentrations than consumers. Densely crowded, poorly ventilated meat packing plants in particular have become COVID-19 hotspots across North America and Europe.

Many people choose to avoid foods produced this way for ethical as well as for health reasons. The exploitation of these workers, as well as the reluctance to discover and implement solutions that could make the food supply safer, shows the degree to which industrial agriculture businesses are prepared to disregard human life and public health.

B

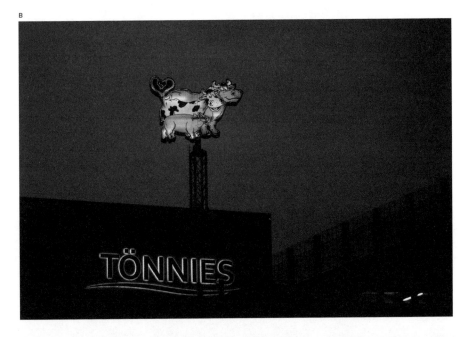

A

When people learn about the global industrial food system and the devastating effects the Standard American or Western diet has on human health and the environment, it often inspires personal change. But the only way forward that benefits everyone is the implementation of rational food policies all around the globe.

This means legislation that governs agricultural subsidies and food assistant programmes must focus on public health goals, not profits for corporations. To get back to health there must be widespread laws that ensure farmers are paid fairly and food workers at all levels are guaranteed common sense safety protections. And, above all, policies must make environmental stewardship and soil conservation the highest priorities to help combat climate change.

On the surface it appears that a universal switch to organic or bio farming would be the perfect solution. It is often assumed that foods with this official imprimatur are automatically more environmentally friendly and healthier, too. It is true that these seals indicate that the foods meet certain legal standards, but they only tell part of the story.

Bio is a term used across the European Union to indicate that food was produced according to EU rules and regulations for organic farming.

B

nach
EG-Öko-Verordnung

A   Workers at a Fairtrade
    coffee farm in Jimma, Ethiopia,
    drying coffee beans in the sun.
B   Clockwise from above left,
    an EU logo for organic farming,
    the Soil Association Organic
    Standard logo, the USDA
    organic logo and the German
    state organic seal.

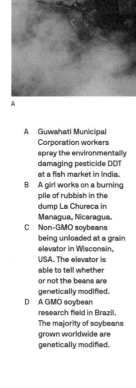

A

B

A Guwahati Municipal Corporation workers spray the environmentally damaging pesticide DDT at a fish market in India.

B A girl works on a burning pile of rubbish in the dump La Chureca in Managua, Nicaragua.

C Non-GMO soybeans being unloaded at a grain elevator in Wisconsin, USA. The elevator is able to tell whether or not the beans are genetically modified.

D A GMO soybean research field in Brazil. The majority of soybeans grown worldwide are genetically modified.

DDT, or dichlorodiphenyl-trichloroethane, was one of the first modern synthetic insecticides.

GMO stands for genetically modified organism.

In the 1960s, Rachel Carson's landmark book *Silent Spring* raised awareness about the problems of pesticides. The book examined, among other things, the damage the pesticide DDT inflicted on bird populations, pointing out to readers that the chemical is carcinogenic. The popularity of the book probably helped lead to the eventual banning of DDT in the United States in 1972 and internationally in 2004. Unfortunately, DDT so profoundly contaminated soil during the time it was used that traces of it persist in today's food supply, especially in meat and dairy; toxic residues concentrate on their way up the food chain.

The book also sparked interest in organic methods of growing food.

C

SOJA INTACTA RR2 PRO
SEM INSETICIDA

D

Modern organic farming is a direct response to the rise of industrial agriculture. As it became standard practice to use synthetic pesticides and fertilizers, farmers and consumers alike wanted an alternative. In organic farming, pests are managed with natural methods. Fertilizer is not a fossil fuel based chemical that is bought from a corporation; it comes from plant and animal waste that occurs on the farm. And nitrogen-fixing cover crops such as legumes enrich the soil and guard against erosion. There are no GMO crops on an organic or bio farm.

The organic food movement was well underway before any regulations were set for farming practices. In the United States, Oregon was first state to codify laws governing organic food in 1973. Other states followed with their own regulations, which differed from one to the next, while many states set no rules around what could be called organic at all. In 1990, the United States Congress set standards for what food could bear the label USDA organic. The European Union has regulated organically produced food since 1991, and many other countries also have systems in place.

As the demand for organic food has grown, so have organic farms themselves. Unfortunately, this means that today, a considerable segment of organic food production overlaps with industrial farming and shares some, if not all, of its problems.

Organic romaine, grown over vast fields in the same two regions as non-organic romaine, have not been spared from E. coli contamination or recalls. A 2015 study from the University of Washington suggests that industrial-scale organic farming operations actually emit more greenhouse gases than similar conventional farms. Restoring food production health is not so simple.

A

B

For some farmers and consumers, the term organic has become all but meaningless. Heavily processed 'organic' junk food fills the aisles of gourmet supermarkets while small farmers whose practices exceed the set government standards do not receive the official seal, either because it is meaningless to them, or the costs incurred by pursuing the certification are prohibitive.

A Farm workers (clockwise from top left) planting produce, harvesting fresh corn cobs at a community-sponsored organic farm, feeding livestock with oats, wheat and peas and filling a trough for cows.

B Snack food giants try to capitalize on the health halo that comes with the label 'organic', as seen on the branding of these Garden of Eatin' tortilla chips, Doritos tortilla chips and Trader Joe's kale chips. In spite of the health conscious buzzwords on the packaging, crisps are still a processed food.

Government food, agricultural and trade regulations for both organic and conventional farms need to change all over the world for health outcomes to improve significantly at a population level. There will always be bad actors that follow the letter of the law while violating its spirit; this is part of how 'big organic' has chipped away at the meaning of the USDA organic seal. Still, whether the environment becomes or stays obesogenic has everything to do with the laws of the land. It results from value systems that put profits over people.

A

There have been some efforts to move the needle on public policy. In 2018, the United States, formed a congressional 'Food is Medicine' working group charged with coming up with new food and nutritional policies to cut diet-related healthcare costs and make the population healthier overall. Later that year, subsidies for fruits and vegetables for those on public assistance were increased and hundreds of millions of dollars were earmarked for nutrition education programmes. The USDA is in a difficult position, though, as it has the conflicting twin goals of establishing the nation's food guidelines and protecting the financial interests of factory farmers, flooding the market with the very refined carbohydrates and saturated fats that cause deadly diseases, including heart disease, cancer and diabetes.

Other programmes that could help improve health have struggled to get established. For example, an initiative to provide medically-tailored meals in the US went unfunded. There is credible research showing that meal prescription is cheaper than medication, and more effective. In California, a recent study suggests that medically-tailored meals have saved taxpayers $6 million in healthcare costs. Perhaps precision fermentation technology will eventually allow the creation of healthy and tasty foods locally and cheaply, and the design of individualized nutrition, thus improving our health and the health of the planet simultaneously.

In 2004, British chef Jamie Oliver (b. 1975) filmed a TV series documenting his efforts to improve the quality and nutritional value of school dinners at a typical British school. This turned into his high-profile Feed Me Better campaign, targeting the junk food being served in schools across England. The result was a £280 million pledge from the government to tackle the problem, and the introduction of School Food Standards. How widely the new standards are properly implemented is questionable, however, as researchers from the Jamie Oliver Foundation discovered in 2019 that many schools still served high fat and sugar foods, including pizzas, muffins and doughnuts.

Clearly public health programmes and TV chef initiatives may do some good, but they are not enough to stop our food from killing us. A more wholesale and radical approach needs to be taken to make meaningful change.

Medically-tailored meals are custom-prepared meals containing food that supports health for people with particular chronic medical conditions.

B

A The US Food and Drug Administration building at the agency's campus in Silver Spring, Maryland.
B Unhealthy lunches made up of foods including chocolate-flavoured milk, pizza, chips, crisps, burgers doughnuts and chocolate puddings – are common for students in the USA.

A American children drink large quantities of soda at a New York City protest intended to fight a proposed law that would ban sugary drinks in containers larger than 450 grams (16 oz).

B Social media advertising for fast food during the COVID-19 pandemic. Companies sought to turn new trends – such as conference calls or online quizzes – into new opportunities for junk food, and to cash in on people missing the experience of eating out.

Food labelling laws are another example of something in need of an overhaul. Many current food labelling laws contribute to confusion around nutrition and food. Serving sizes, for example, are often expressed in grams, leaving consumers with no concrete idea of how much to eat.

Serving sizes are also frequently at odds with the way products are actually consumed. For example, bottled beverages are usually consumed all at once in a single serving, though they are often labelled as two servings. If you do not carefully read the label on a bottled smoothie, you may easily consume 500 calories thinking it was only 250.

A

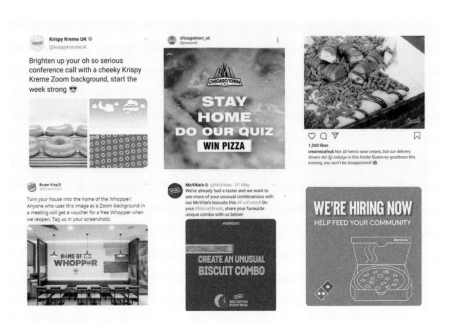

B

And then there is the matter of sugar. Health advocates have pressed for sugar quantities to be labelled in teaspoons instead of grams. Everyone has a clear idea of how many teaspoons they put in their coffee for example, which gives you a frame of reference. You may decide against drinking a pre-sweetened coffee that has 12 teaspoons of sugar (50 grams/1⅘ oz) when you compare it with the coffee you prepare for yourself with only 1 teaspoon (4.2 grams/³⁄₂₀ oz). The World Health Organization advises consuming less than 50 grams (1⅘ oz) of added sugar per day.

Across the board, attempts at progress are regularly thwarted by powerful lobbyists, trade associations, and industry groups. Opposition to food regulations comes primarily from the food industry itself. Soda makers would have you believe that it is lack of exercise and not their calorie-dense, sugar-filled beverages that cause obesity. And they spend big money to push their agendas. In 2017 the Obesity Health Alliance found that the companies producing the UK's top 18 food brands had spent more than £143 million advertising their products in the past year. This was compared to the £5.2 million spent by the government on their flagship healthy eating campaign Change4Life.

| Eggs | Butter | Milk | | Meat | | Seafood | | Bakery |

Cheese

Bulk

Frozen | Frozen | Beverages | Water | Coffee | Tea | Cereal | Baked Goods | Chips | Condiments | Canned Foods | Grains | Baking | Spices | Oil | Deli | Veg. | Vegetables

Fruits

Wine | Spirits | Checkout | Fruits | Floral

A

In 2010 a proposed 'traffic light' system for food labels to indicate the levels of salt, fat and other nutrients in each product was rejected by the EU, following a multimillion-pound lobbying campaign by food manufacturers. Independent research had revealed consumers found the system the easiest way to make informed choices. Traffic light systems could very well help to reduce obesity levels around the world. Industry insists it can police itself, and that voluntary efforts are more effective than laws. Industry is clearly wrong.

So, while you are embracing your role as food activist to help force the Big Food and big agriculture industries to change and bring about bold new policies to transform the obesogenic environment, is there anything you can do to help yourself be healthy? Yes. Just know you will be continually swimming upstream. The industrial food system is set up to make such changes expensive, difficult, time consuming and outside of social norms.

Cigarettes | Spirits		Wine	Water	Herbs | Spices	

Check out	Fruit | Vegetables	Tea | Coffee | Seeds | Nuts | Chips			Confectionery
		Household	Toiletries	Bakery	
		Lean Meat	Oily Fish	Ready Meals	
		Sandwiches | Soft Drinks			

Milk | Yoghurt | Cheese	Beans | Pulses | Eggs	Demonstration Area
Potatoes | Rice | Bread | Cereal | Pasta		
Fruit | Vegetables		

→

B

A   This graphic represents a classic supermarket layout, in which whole foods, including meat, fruit and vegetables, can generally be found around the perimeter of the shop.

B   This graphic represents a redesigned supermarket layout to encourage healthier eating. Greater prominence is given to fruit and vegetables, and it is easier to avoid ready meals, snacks, sweets, soft drinks and alcohol.

A nutritious diet starts with shopping. There are those who would say that typical supermarkets around the world do not sell 'real food'. And it is true that when you combine all the household products, such as paper towels and shampoos, with aisle upon aisle of ultra-processed foods such as crisps, soda and breakfast cereal, you have covered most of the floor area in a typical supermarket. However, there is a way to navigate these stores to make it more likely that you will find the 'real food' and make better choices: you need to focus on the perimeter of the store.

It is at the edges where you will find all the produce as well as fresh meat and dairy – that is where the refrigerated cases are. Things that are shelf-stable for eternity, such as soda and biscuits, inhabit the space in the middle of the store. Of course, you will need to strategically visit those centre aisles. That is where you will find canned beans and whole wheat pasta after all. But the perimeter should be where you spend most of your time and money at a supermarket.

Community Supported Agriculture Programmes (CSAs) are subscription programmes where a customer pays up front at the time of planting for a share of a farm's crops throughout the growing season. A similar system in Japan called Teikei has existed since the 1960s.

A

A   Whether motivated by the high cost of fresh food or a desire to reduce food waste, this dumpster diver picks through discarded food items at the back of a supermarket in Berlin, Germany. Below are the edible food items retrieved from the rubbish.
B   A volunteer fills up boxes with produce at Fruta Feia (Ugly Fruit) in Lisbon, Portugal. The co-op was created to save the produce that does not meet supermarket standards.

The fresh groceries you need for optimal health are also more expensive than processed food, presenting a socioeconomic barrier to eating well. Even having access to a grocery store cannot be taken as given. Many people around the world live in food deserts, areas with limited access to fresh, nutritious food. Families in these areas often shop at corner and convenience shops where little to no produce is sold.

If you are able to do so, shopping at local farmers' markets is a good way to access higher quality local food and bolster your local economy. Farmers' markets have proliferated during the past decade, with an increasing focus on 'producers-only' markets, where all the vendors are growing or making what they sell. This is the perfect forum to learn more about farming in your community by talking to the farmers themselves. You can ask them how they handle pest management and what they use for fertilizer. You can find out how they care for their land, what their animals eat and how they are slaughtered.

If you find a farm you love, if you can afford it, you may want to sign up for its community supported agriculture programme (CSA). In this business model, a farm sells shares of its whole seasonal harvest ahead of time. You pay in advance of the growing season, and then receive a weekly box of farm-fresh vegetables. It is a wonderful way to ensure you eat a greater variety of fresh vegetables. It also lets you support your favourite farm directly as the kind of farming practices you believe in.

'Ugly produce' programmes work in a similar way to CSAs. Subscribers receive a large box of 'ugly' vegetables every week. Instead of coming from a single farm, the food in these boxes represents perfectly good produce that falls short of supermarket's cosmetic standards for produce. This could mean apples that are small, carrots that have a peculiar shape, lemons that are not quite the right colour. Not only do these programmes help you eat more vegetables, they also help cut food waste by selling at a discount produce that may otherwise have been discarded.

B

It can be very hard to continue eating conventional meat when you have learned about factory farming, its devastating toll on the planet, and the appalling conditions in which livestock lives and dies. Additionally, if your food budget is tight, cutting down on meat or eliminating it entirely can be an excellent way to increase the money you have to spend on healthier foods.

If you cannot imagine switching to a vegetarian diet, you can still choose to opt out of the factory farmed meat system. Many communities offer cow- or pig-share programmes that invite shoppers to buy a percentage of a whole animal directly from a local farm. It costs a lot up front, but if you can make the investment, it is a good value over time in terms of the price you pay per pound. The meat arrives pre-packed and frozen. Even one-eighth of a cow will last a family a long time if they are eating a plant-based diet.

A

Food co-ops are community-owned grocery stores, often specializing in healthy, whole-food ingredients and operating at cost.

A   The Park Slope Food Co-op in Park Slope, Brooklyn, New York. Established in 1973, it is one of the oldest and largest active food co-operatives in the USA. Co-op members must work periodic shifts at the grocery store in order to shop there.
B   A volunteer gardener and homeless man works at an urban and community garden near Madrid, Spain.

Food co-ops, where they exist, are another good choice for shoppers wanting to know more about the origin and quality of their food. Member-owned, these smaller grocery stores typically stock plenty of healthy staples such as dried beans and whole grains, often sold in bulk, and focus on supporting the local economy.

Increasingly, co-ops place special emphasis on offering plenty of low-priced wholesome staples so no one in the community is excluded for financial reasons. Other food co-ops remain inaccessible to people with lower incomes. But if you can do it, joining a co-op and shopping there is a wonderful way to vote with your cash for the kind of food system you think would be healthier for people and the planet.

Better yet, if you have a garden or access to community garden, growing your own food can be an affordable way to fill your refrigerator with fresh, healthy produce while giving yourself a degree of self-sufficiency from the food system.

A

If overhauling both your entire diet and the way you shop for food feels overwhelming that is because it is. However, you do not need to make immediate sweeping changes to the way you live to start working towards establishing a more nutritious diet.

You have probably heard the term 'clean eating'. It's a controversial one, ascribing undue moral virtue to a style of eating, but it can be a useful shorthand for the type of diet that is dramatically less likely to kill you than the modern Western diet.

So for our purposes, 'clean eating' refers to a diet dominated by non-factory farmed vegetables, legumes, fruits and whole grains, with dairy, meat and fish as optional extras, in moderation, and with minimal processed foods. You may know this style of eating by another name: the Mediterranean diet, often hailed as the 'healthiest diet in the world'.

If you want to make gradual changes to bring your diet more in line with the healthiest diet in the world, here are five key steps to get you started:

Clean eating is a term used to describe a diet that minimizes processed food. It is misused by some to advocate for a highly restrictive diet based on pseudo-science.

The **Mediterranean diet** is high in vegetables, fruit, whole grains, fish and unsaturated fats, and low in meat and diary products. The diet is given this name as it is traditionally practised by people from countries bordering the Mediterranean Sea, including France, Greece, Italy and Spain. Research has consistently linked it with reduced risk of cardiovascular diseases.

B

C

A

A **flexitarian** diet is a plant-based diet that is flexible. It limits processed foods and sugar, and allows the occasional incorporation of meat and diary products.

A   Canned sodas and lengthy ingredients lists have a very limited place in a diet that promotes health.

B   Unprocessed whole foods, such as broccoli and beans, get the green light from nutritionists.

Stop drinking soda. Fizzy drinks, both diet and regular, do nothing for your health. Typically sweetened with high fructose corn syrup, soda or other sweetened drink consumption is closely correlated with obesity. It is typical for soda drinkers to consume 200 or more extra calories a day. And research from the Johns Hopkins Bloomberg School of Public Health shows that those who choose diet drinks end up consuming even more calories than their peers who drink sugar-sweetened soda. This is probably because your body detects sweetness and expects calories. When the diet soda does not provide them, the body finds them elsewhere.

Eat more vegetables. Once you have conquered sodas, it is time to turn your attention to vegetables. According to Eurostat, in 2014 only 14 per cent of EU members ate five or more portions of fruit and vegetables per day, and according to the CDC in 2017 only 10 per cent of Americans meet the guidelines for the recommended amount of fruit and vegetables in a day. Making a salad to go with lunch or dinner is one simple way to eat more veg. A second side dish of simply roasted vegetables like broccoli or cauliflower can also help you meet your goals.

B

Cut back on meat and dairy. Not only are these foods filled with saturated fat, their production is exceptionally tough on the environment. Many people cannot afford the responsibly produced, grass-fed meat and diary due to cost. Try going meatless on Mondays or going 'flexitarian'. Swap beef burgers for veggie burgers.

Add beans and whole grains. As with fruits and vegetables, few people get the recommended amount of fibre in their diet. The fastest way to increase fibre intake is to add beans and whole grains to your diet. Try swapping quinoa for rice or pasta and try to make beans a daily part of your diet. Hummus is a great way to do it. Eat it with vegetable sticks or whole grain pita for a fibre bonus.

Eliminate ultra-processed food. Highly processed foods, packed with sugar, salt and fat, are perhaps the biggest threat in the modern obesogenic environment. Start reading ingredients lists: when it is long and contains many items you cannot pronounce and do not stock in your kitchen, you know you are dealing with an ultra-processed food. The food served at fast food restaurants also falls into this category. The less of it you eat, the healthier you will be.

An increasingly popular way to evade all the deadliest parts of the Western diet and the industrial food system is to embrace a plant-based diet. The plant-based diet is exactly what it sounds like: you mostly eat plant foods, adding meat and diary only occasionally, or not at all. That may sound restrictive, but this is a category of food with stunning variety within it. As you may recall from Chapter Two, on the whole human beings obtain 60 per cent of their calories from only three plants. There are so many more delicious plants out there waiting to be eaten.

A

B

A Environmental, animal welfare and health advocates all believe the future must be plant based.
B A variety of fresh tomatoes at a newly refurbished Marks & Spencer food hall in 2019 in the UK. The new shops feature 50% more fresh produce lines, and 40% more loose varieties of fruit and vegetables.
C This chart shows the feed required to produce 1 kilogram (2⅕ lb) of various meat and dairy products.

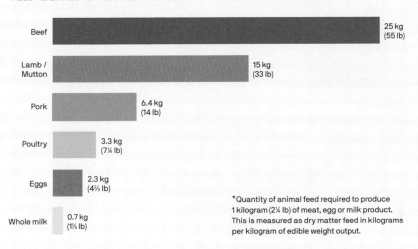

FEED REQUIRED TO PRODUCE ONE KILOGRAM OF MEAT OR DAIRY PRODUCT*

Beef — 25 kg (55 lb)

Lamb / Mutton — 15 kg (33 lb)

Pork — 6.4 kg (14 lb)

Poultry — 3.3 kg (7¼ lb)

Eggs — 2.3 kg (4⅗ lb)

Whole milk — 0.7 kg (1⅗ lb)

*Quantity of animal feed required to produce 1 kilogram (2¼ lb) of meat, egg or milk product. This is measured as dry matter feed in kilograms per kilogram of edible weight output.

c

The staples of plant-based diets include all the vegetables (including starchy, filling potatoes and sweet potatoes) and fruits; grains in all their whole and ground glory; beans and legumes (as of this writing, the heirloom bean seller Rancho Gordo offers 31 varieties on its website); and nuts and seeds (a very convincing cream alternative can be made from cashews). It is common for people on plant-based diets to consume a drastically wider variety of foods than those who eat a meat-centric one. If preventing the deadliest chronic diseases including heart disease and diabetes is your goal, the research behind plant-based diets is persuasive.

There is concern that without the industrial food system, it would be impossible to feed the world. But this worry often does not take into consideration how many more calories would be available for people if we were not using most of the food we grow as animal feed. Scientists have estimated that the United States alone could feed 800 million people with the grains used to raise livestock. And this is to say nothing of the water required. Dairy cows drink up to 230 litres (50 gallons) a day, and that does not even include the water used to grow the feed they eat daily.

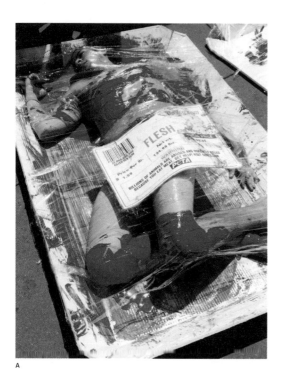

A

A Many people chose a vegan diet for ethical reasons, such as this participant in PETA's 2010 'Meat is Murder' demonstration in Times Square, New York, USA.

B Clockwise from top left: delivery drivers demanding better employment rights and safety in Italy; a demonstration against 'fake food' in Taipei, Taiwan; a protest against the TTIP and CETA free trade agreements in Germany, which protesters believe pose threats to food safety, corporate accountability and consumer protection; and Greenpeace activists demanding improved food safety legislation in Hong Kong.

A plant-based whole foods diet is not the same as a vegan diet, a term that has been in circulation for generations. A vegan diet places a great emphasis on what you do not eat and its adherents are often as motivated by the ill treatment of animals as their own health. A plant-based diet places more emphasis on what you do eat, and of course, your diet's impact on your health. Many people who embrace plant-based diets do so with a flexible mindset that allows for exceptions.

The good news is you do not have to be fully plant-based to begin protecting yourself from the chronic diseases brought on by the modern Western diet. The more plant-based your diet becomes, the more you will reduce your risks.

A whole foods plant-based diet is not an all or nothing proposition, which is why it has become popular with more and more people. Allow yourself some responsibly sourced fish and meat occasionally, or some soy-based chicken or veggie burgers.

If you have the information, financial resources, and time to tackle these dietary changes, you are likely among the most privileged people on the planet. Most global citizens cannot take this proactive approach and will remain at the mercy of the obesogenic environment until food and social justice activists demand leaders and policies that prioritize creating a global food system that is safe and healthy for everyone.

Conclusion

A

The realities of our broken, global, industrial food system can really make you lose your appetite. Almost any food choice can set off a series of questions and considerations that could turn anyone's stomach. Remember, whole-person health is about more than simply what you eat. Your mental health is also important, and so is managing stress and maintaining connections with your family and community, which often involves shared meals.

The term 'orthorexia' was coined in the late 1990s to describe an obsession with healthy eating that interferes with a person's ability to live their normal lives. It is not a coincidence that this disorder rose to awareness amidst the breakdown of traditional foodways and the rise of ultra-processed foods. While our food on the whole may indeed be killing us, anxieties and obsession around eating do not have to take a toll on our wellbeing, too.

Obesity is an epidemic, but fatphobia is a crisis as well. It is possible to look for ways to address obesity on a population scale while supporting individuals living with obesity and respecting their humanity. Weight bias, especially in medicine, needs to be eliminated. And if you are living in a larger body, it can be particularly difficult to stay sane about food because you feel that everything you eat is scrutinized by the world at large.

One way to promote sanity around food is to resist diet culture. Diet culture refers to the incessant promotion of weight loss programmes and glorification of weight loss that is everywhere in the media. Even if you would like to lose weight, it is healthier to approach it from a true lifestyle change perspective, placing your focus on health behaviours with the goal of losing weight as secondary. Research shows that gradual weight loss has a better chance of lasting the rest of your life than the swift weight loss seen on reality TV.

A Modern culture has made gatherings such as the traditional English family Sunday lunch less common.

B British activist Jameela Jamil's Instagram story. She denounces the fact that women are encouraged to view themselves through the lens of weight, weight loss and diet culture, and promotes the idea that women should instead value themselves through their relationships, achievements and interests.

Some maintain that the modern agricultural system is needed to feed our global population. However, currently with this system more than 820 million people worldwide do not have food security, that is, reliable access to enough nutritious food to meet their needs. In addition, agriculture is responsible for 10 – 12 per cent of greenhouse gas emissions, with livestock an extremely inefficient use of land. Of the 5 billion hectares of agricultural land on the planet today, almost 70 per cent is used to graze or grow feed for livestock; it is one of the main drivers of deforestation. Many experts believe that a switch to sustainable agricultural systems could feed the world, particularly if global eating patterns shift to minimize or eliminate animal products.

New business models are advancing alternative food systems by revitalizing food distribution to get produce from farms to consumers at a lower price point with the help of technology. Community food hubs and forward-thinking business have used apps and the Internet to help connect buyers with farmers, creating efficiencies that can bring down the price of local food. Meanwhile, advocates of industrial agriculture believe we need even more proprietary, high-tech innovations in the vein of inorganic fertilizers and GMO crops to feed a growing population.

A

A   Giant plastic greenhouses used for intensive agricultural cultivation in Spain.
B   An urban farmer in Los Angeles, California, USA, harvests lettuce to sell to restaurant chefs and consumers via a community-supported agriculture programme (CSA).

B

In *Rethinking Humanity* (2020), James Arbib and Tony Seba go much further. They argue that our food system is already struggling to meet demand and that a reduction of meat and dairy consumption on the scale required to solve climate change is unachievable. Instead they argue for more investment in biological precision technologies and a completely new creation-based and locally organized food production system.

Instead of growing and rearing plants and animals and using elements from them to provide food, the new creation model will construct foods from precisely designed molecules and cells, using the DNA of plants and animals. Proteins, lipids, fibre and vitamins could all be engineered precisely, including nutrition, taste, colour and texture. This will allow scientists, molecular chefs and food designers to develop individual nutrition to suit specific health needs.

Arbib and Seba estimate that by 2035 the cost of producing proteins using biological precision technologies would be 10 times cheaper than the current cost of producing animal proteins, resulting in a 50 per cent reduction in the number of cows raised in the US, for example. They predict that 70 per cent of agricultural land and water would thus be freed up for other uses, including reforestation. The food production system would become completely decentralized in this new model, with a global network of local precision fermentation production hubs set up, slashing the number of food miles that would need to be travelled.

A   Students learn about agriculture on a school field trip to a small farm.

B   Proposed packaging for beef produced using in vitro cell culture of animal cells. Enivronmental and health advocates are hopeful for the future of 'lab grown' meat, as it offers a way to enjoy eating meat without the animal cruelty or environmental damage currently associated with the industry.

C   A busy farmers' market in San Francisco, California, USA.

Many food companies are already developing cultured meat products, cultivating chicken, beef and pork from animal cells. In December 2020 US company Eat Just was the first company to receive regulatory authority to sell lab-grown meat; their 'chicken bites' will be sold in a restaurant in Singapore. Eat Just's cultured chicken uses cells taken from a live animal and grows them in a 1,200-litre (264-gal) bioreactor before combining them with plant-based ingredients. Many companies developing cultured meat products predict that as production is scaled up, cultured meat will produce lower emissions, use far less water and land and be cheaper to buy than conventional meat.

On a personal level, if you eat the way most people around you are eating, you are increasing your risk of developing the diseases of the modern Western diet – obesity, diabetes and heart disease. These diseases are some of the most common killers of our time, and they are up to 80 per cent preventable.

To reduce your risk, you need to be willing to rebel against prevailing cultural norms about eating. Making active choices about what to eat means going against the grain. It can mean shopping at the food co-op and investing in groceries now instead of prescriptions later. It can mean being the odd man out when your friends want to hit up the drive through. It can mean trying new cultured meat products. You need to decide for yourself, based on the best information you have, what your food values are and develop the fortitude to live by them.

To keep our food from killing us, as a global community, we need to become engaged in activism, advocacy and politics, voting for the kind of food supply, food production and environment we want. Unsustainable in its current form, the global food system is a complex one. Changing it will mean making different personal choices, facilitating the safe development of biological technologies and the establishment of new business models. If we do all that it is entirely possible that over the next 10 years or so we will see the demise of our current polluting Big Food system and the rise of a clean, creation-based local food network alongside small-scale organic food producers.

c

Further Reading

Ackerman-Leist, Philip, *Rebuilding the Foodshed: How to Create Local, Sustainable, and Secure Food Systems* (White River Junction, VT: Chelsea Green Publishing, 2013)

Arbib, James and Seba, Tony, *Rethinking Humanity* (San Francisco, CA: RethinkX, 2020)

Barber, Dan, *The Third Plate: Field Notes on the Future of Food* (New York, NY: Penguin Press, 2014)

Campbell, Thomas C. and Campbell, Thomas M., *The China Study: Revised and Expanded Edition: The Most Comprehensive Study of Nutrition Ever Conducted and the Startling Implications for Diet, Weight Loss, and Long-Term Health* (New York, NY: BenBella Books, 2016)

Carson, Rachel, *Silent Spring: Anniversary Edition* (New York, NY: Houghton Mifflin Company, 2002)

Estabrook, Barry, *Tomatoland: How Modern Industrial Agriculture Destroyed Our Most Alluring Fruit* (New York, NY: Andrews McMeel Publishing, 2011)

Foer, Jonathan Safran, *Eating Animals* (New York, NY: Little Brown and Company, 2009)

Fromartz, Samuel, *Organic, Inc.: Natural Foods and How They Grew* (New York, NY: Mariner Books, 2007)

Fung, Jason, *The Obesity Code: Unlocking the Secrets of Weight Loss* (Vancouver: Greystone Books, 2016)

Genoways, Ted, *The Chain: Farm, Factory, and the Fate of Our Food* (New York, NY: Harper, 2014)

Greger, Michael, *How Not to Die: Discover the Foods Scientifically Proven to Prevent and Reverse Disease* (London: Bluebird, 2016)

Herz, Rachel, *Why You Eat What You Eat: The Science Behind our Relationship with Food* (New York, NY: W.W. Norton & Company, 2019)

Hewitt, Ben, *The Town That Food Saved: How One Community Found Vitality in Local Food* (New York, NY: Rodale, 2010)

Kaufman, Frederick, *Bet the Farm: How Food Stopped Being Food* (New York, NY: Wiley, 2012)

Kessler, David A., *The End of Overeating: Taking Control of the Insatiable American Appetite* (New York, NY: Rodale, 2009)

Lappé, Anna, *Diet for a Hot Planet: The Climate Crisis at the End of Your Fork and What You Can Do About it* (New York, NY: Bloomsbury USA, 2010)

Lawless, Kristin, *Formerly Known as Food: How the Industrial Food System Is Changing Our Minds, Bodies, and Culture* (New York, NY: St. Martin's Press, 2018)

McKenna, Maryn, *How Antibiotics Created Modern Agriculture and Changed the Way the World Eats* (Washington, DC: National Geographic Society, 2014)

Moss, Michael, *Salt, Sugar, Fat: How the Food Giants Hooked Us* (New York, NY: Random House, 2014)

Nestle, Marion, *Food Politics, How the Food Industry Influences Nutrition and Health* (Berkeley, CA: University of California Press, 2013)

Nestle, Marion, *The Unsavory Truth: How Food Companies Skew the Science of What We Eat* (New York, NY: Basic Books, 2018)

Nestle, Marion, *What to Eat* (New York, NY: North Point Press, 2007)

Patel, Raj, *Stuffed and Starved: Markets, Power and the Hidden Battle for the World Food System* (London: Melville House, 2012)

Petrini, Carlo, *Slow Food Nation: Why Our Food Should Be Good, Clean, and Fair* (New York, NY: Rizzoli Ex Libris, 2005)

Pollan, Michael, *Cooked: A Natural History of Transformation* (New York, NY: Penguin, 2013)

Pollan, Michael, *Food Rules: An Eater's Manual* (New York, NY: Penguin, 2009)

Pollan, Michael, *In Defense of Food: An Eater's Manifesto* (New York, NY: Penguin, 2009)

Pollan, Michael, *The Omnivore's Dilemma: A Natural History of Four Meals* (New York, NY: Penguin, 2006)

Pringle, Peter, *Food Inc.: Medel to Monsanto—The Promises and Perils of the Biotech Harvest* (New York, NY: Simon & Schuster, 2003)

Robbins, John, *The Food Revolution: How Your Diet Can Help Save Your Life and Our World* (New York, NY: Conari Press, 2001)

Rodale, Maria, *Organic Manifesto: How Organic Farming Can Heal Our Planet, Feed the World, and Keep Us Safe* (New York, NY: Rodale, 2010)

Schatzker, Mark, *The Dorito Effect: The Surprising New Truth About Food and Flavor* (New York, NY: Simon & Schuster, 2015)

Schlosser, Eric, *Fast Food Nation: The Dark Side of the All-American Meal* (New York, NY: Harper Perennial, 2005)

Simon, David Robinson, *Meatonomics: How the Rigged Economics of Meat and Dairy Make You Consume Too Much— and How to Eat Better, Live Longer, and Spend Smarter* (New York, NY: Conari Press 2013)

Simon, Michele, *Appetite for Profit: How the Food Industry Undermines Our Health and How to Fight Back* (New York, NY: Bold Type Books, 2006)

Spurlock, Morgan, *Don't Eat This Book: Fast Food and the Supersizing of America* (New York, NY: G. P. Putnam's Sons, 2005)

Vileisis, Ann, *Kitchen Literacy: How We Lost Knowledge of Where Food Comes from and Why We Need to Get It Back* (New York, NY: Island Press, 2007)

Warner, Melanie, *Pandora's Lunchbox: How Processed Food Took Over the American Meal* (New York, NY: Scribner, 2013)

Weber, Karl, *Food Inc: A Participant Guide: How Industrial Food is Making Us Sicker, Fatter, and Poorer – And What You Can Do About It* (New York, NY: Public Affairs, 2009)

Wilson, Bee, *The Way We Eat Now: Strategies for Eating in a World of Change* (New York, NY: Fourth Estate, 2019)

Picture Credits

Every effort has been made to locate and credit copyright holders of the material reproduced in this book. The author and publisher apologize for any omissions or errors, which can be corrected in future editions.

a = above, b = below, c = centre, l = left, r = right

2 Engineer studio
4–5 Chones
6–7 MaxyM
8 Chris McGrath/ Getty Images
9a Alex Wong/Getty Images
9b Tengku Bahar/AFP/ Getty Images
10 Thames & Hudson
12 Miquel Benitez/Getty Images
13a Thomas Trutschel/ Photothek via Getty Images
13b Natalia Fedosenko/ Tass via Getty Images
15 Wan Zhen/VCG via Getty Images
16a Charlie Neibergall/AP/ Shutterstock
16b Mahmut Serdar Alakus/ Anadolu Agency via Getty Images
17a Qilai Shen/Bloomberg via Getty Images
17b Luke Sharrett/Bloomberg via Getty Images
18 Alexander Ryumin/ Tass via Getty Images
19 MJ Photography/ Alamy Stock Photo
20–1 © Martin Parr/ Magnum Photos
22 Kevin Frayer/ Getty Images
23 Thames & Hudson
24 Philippe Desmazes/ AFP via Getty Images
25l Sipa/Shutterstock
25r © Martin Parr/ Magnum Photos
26 NCD Risk Factor

Collaboration, www.ncdrisc.org
27 Raul Arboleda/ AFP via Getty Images
28 Granger/Shutterstock
29 Private Collection
30 Everett/Shutterstock
31al Hemis/Alamy Stock Photo
31ar Forrest Anderson/The LIFE Images Collection via Getty Images
31bl Vahid Salemi/AP/ Shutterstock
31br Greg Baker/AP/ Shutterstock
32 Royal Foods
33 John Dominis/The LIFE Picture Collection via Getty Images
34 Lightspring
35 Chantal Garnier/ Unsplash
36 Content supplied by the world's largest charitable funder of cancer research, © Cancer Research UK 2019. All rights reserved.
37 Maureen McLean/ Alamy Stock Photo
38 Nikki Kahn/The Washington Post via Getty Images
39 Thames & Hudson
40 Jay Directo/AFP via Getty Images
41a Jeffrey Isaac Greenberg 15+/Alamy Stock Photo
41b Justin Kase zsixz/ Alamy Stock Photo
42–3 Behrouz Mehri/AFP via Getty Images
44–5 Louis Quail/In Pictures via Getty Images
46–7 Peter Bond/Unsplash
48 D. Corson/ClassicStock/ Getty Images
49 Zuidhof M.J., Schneider B.L., Carney V.L., Korver D.R. and Robinson F.E. 'Growth, efficiency, and yield of commercial broilers from 1957, 1978, and 2005'. Poult Sci. 2014

50l Bob Berg/Getty Images
50r Chris McGrath/ Getty Images
51 Dario Pignatelli/ Bloomberg via Getty Images
52 Yeti studio
53 Sugarstacks.com
54l Photofusion/ Shutterstock
54c Paul Sakuma/AP/ Shutterstock
54r Richard Levine/ Alamy Stock Photo
55l Pictorial Press Ltd/ Alamy Stock Photo
55r Private Collection
56l Kitamin
56r A StockStudio
57l Kitamin
57r Bigacis
58l Instagram/Kim Kardashian
58r Instagram/Kylie Jenner
59 Geoffrey Robinson/ Shutterstock
60 Lawrence Welkowitz/ Canvas
61 Peangdao
62–3 Patrik Stollarz/AFP via Getty Images
64 Brent Lewin/Bloomberg via Getty Images
65 Sara Stathas/ Alamy Stock Photo
66 Alibaba
67a Marek Slusarczyk/ Alamy Stock Photo
67b Andy Gibson/ Alamy Stock Photo
68 Bored Panda
69 Bob Riha, Jr./Nintendo of America via Getty Images
70a Reuters/Alamy Stock Photo
70b Fernando Vergara/AP/ Shutterstock
71a J R Ripper/Brazil Photos/ LightRocket via Getty Images
71b Joshua Paul/Bloomberg/ Getty Images
72 Daniel Acker/Bloomberg via Getty Images
73 Yang Min/VCG

via Getty Images
74l, c Michael Neelon(misc)/
Alamy Stock Photo
74r Ben Molyneux/
Alamy Stock Photo
75 Thames & Hudson
76 Justin Sullivan/
Getty Images
77 Anusak Laowilas/
NurPhoto via Getty
Images
78–9 Christopher Furlong/
Getty Images
80l Faisal Khan/Zuma Wire/
Shutterstock
80r Nicolas Tucat/
AFP via Getty Images
81l Tim Marsden/EPA-EFE/
Shutterstock
81r Jerome Favre/EPA/
Shutterstock
82 Carbon Trust
83l Creative Touch Imaging
Ltd./NurPhoto
via Getty Images
83r Jessica Rinaldi/
The Boston Globe
via Getty Images
84a Neil Guegan/Alamy
Stock Photo
84b Mihai Andritoiu/
Alamy Stock Photo
85a nsf/Alamy Stock Photo
85b U.S. National
Archives and Records
Administration
86 Seyllou/AFP
via Getty Images
87l Philip Scalia/
Alamy Stock Photo
87c Bildagentur-online/
Ohde/Alamy Stock Photo
87r Citizen of the Planet/
Alamy Stock Photo
88 Shutterstock
89a Jasper Juinen/Bloomberg
via Getty Images
89b Joel Saget/AFP via Getty
Images
90a Ben Curtis/AP/
Shutterstock
90b Mohamed El-Shahed/
AFP via Getty Images
91 Stefano Montesi/Corbis
via Getty Images
92a BSIP/UIG
via Getty Images

92b BSIP/Universal Images
Group via Getty Images
93 Jim West/Alamy
Stock Photo
94a John Macdougall/
AFP via Getty Images
94b Christopher Furlong/
Getty Images
95 Robert Browman/
Getty Images
96a Mike Kemp/In Pictures
via Getty Images
96b Robert F Bukaty/AP/
Shutterstock
97 Michael Urban/DDP/
AFP via Getty Images
98 Sean Gallup/Getty
Images
99 Andrew Caballero-
Reynolds/AFP
via Getty Images
100 Centers for Disease
Control and Prevention,
U.S. Department of Health
& Human Services
101 Lukas Schulze/
Getty Images
102–3 Brigitte Blättler
104 Eric Lafforgue/Art in
All of Us/Corbis via
Getty Images
105al European Commission
105ar Soil Association
105bl USDA
105br Bio-Siegel
106l David Talukdar/
Shutterstock
106r Jan Sochor/
Latincontent/
Getty Images
107l Scott Olson/
Getty Images
107r Paulo Fridman/
Bloomberg via
Getty Images
108al Michael Rougier/The
LIFE Picture Collection
via Getty Images
108ar Ralf-Finn Hestoft/
CORBIS/Corbis
via Getty Images
108bl, Stevens Frémont/Sygma
br via Getty Images
109l Keith Homan/
Alamy Stock Photo
109c Michael Neelon(misc)/
Alamy Stock Photo

109r Ed Endicott/Alamy
Stock Photo
110 Jacquelyn Martin/
AP/Shutterstock
111a DebbiSmirnoff
111b kcline
112 Reuters/Andrew Burton
113 Obesity Health Alliance
114–5 Thames & Hudson
116 John Macdougall/
AFP via Getty Images
117 Patricia De Melo Moreira/
AFP via Getty Images
118a Keith Getter/
Getty Images
118b Chris Hondros/
Getty Images
119 Dani Pozo/AFP
via Getty Images
120 Chatelaine
121a © Marco Bottigelli
121b Klaus Vedfelt
122l Jasper Juinen/Bloomberg
via Getty Images
122r Michael Neelon/
Alamy Stock Photo
123l s_derevianko
123r MOAimage
124a Dave Rushen/SOPA
Images/Shutterstock
124b Hollie Adams/Bloomberg
via Getty Images
125 Thames & Hudson
126 Ben Gabbe/Getty Images
127al Michele Lapini/
Getty Images
127ar Sam Yeh/AFP
via Getty Images
127bl Mike Clarke/AFP
via Getty Images
127br Clemens Bilan/
Getty Images
128–9 ©Paul Langrock/
Greenpeace
130 ©Chris Steele-Perkins/
Magnum Photos
131 Instagram/Jameela Jamil
132 David Ramos/Bloomberg
via Getty Images
133 Robyn Beck/AFP
via Getty Images
134a Universal Images
Group via Getty Images
134b Firn/Alamy Stock Photo
135 David Paul Morris/
Bloomberg via Getty
Images

Index

References to illustrations
are in **bold**.

acid reflux 44, 45
activism 114–15, **124**, **126**, 127,
   131, 135
addiction 54
ADHD 91
advertising
   children 69
   compared to reality **68**, 69
   diets **58**, 59
   eggs **55**
   fast food **54**, 112, **113**
   psychology 68–9
   public health programmes
   113
   regulation 69, 77
   social media **58** 59
   volume 68, 113
agribusinesses 75, 84, 101
agriculture see also farms
   'big' 28, **29**, 52
   community supported (CSA)
   116, 117, **133**
   industrialization 11–16, **18**,
   28, 48, **49**, 71–4, 80–1, 95,
   108, **132**, 133 see also
   factory farms
   production growth 84
algae blooms **88**, 89
American Medical
   Association 25
animal feed 50, 74
antibiotic resistance 92–3
antibiotics 14, 15, 91–2
Arbib, James 133–4
avocados 82

bacteria 63, 91–2, 94–8
bananas **70**, 71
beans 60, **61**, 123
beverages
   availability **41**
   bliss point 53
   consumption reduction 122
   diet drinks 121
   intake levels **10**, 11

main companies 30
portion sizes 112
soda taxes 30, 76
sugar levels 76, 113
big agriculture 28, **29**, 52
Big Food 12, 51, 62, 74, 114
bio, as regulatory term 105
biodiversity loss 18, 19, 70–1, 88
biofuel 74
bisphenol A (BPA) 62, 64
bliss point 52, 53
blood pressure, high 10, 11, 34
blood sugar 35
body mass index (BMI) 22, **23**,
   24
body size 58
brain
   advertising 68, 69
   food effects 55–7
breakfast 54–5
broiler chickens 17, 50
burgers 28, **29**, 59–60
business models 133, 135
butylated hydroxyanisole (BHA)
   66, 67
butylated hydroxytoluene (BHT)
   62, 66

Cadbury Schweppes 53
CAFOs (concentrated animal
   feeding operations) 16, 17,
   93, 95
calorie sources
   beverages 122
   income relationship 38, **39**
   staple foods 71
'calories in, calories out' 58–9
cancer
   BHT & BHA 66
   definition 11
   diet 10, 33, 36, 37
   glyphosate 89
   obesity 24, 36–7
   processed meats 17
canned foods 28, **64–5**
carbon footprint 82, **84**, 85
carcinogens 16, 17, 89, 90, 106
Carson, Rachel 106
celebrities **58**, 59
cereals

high-yielding varieties
   (HYVs) 14
   nutrition 17
chemicals in farming 14
   see also fertilizers;
   herbicides; pesticides
chickens
   bacterial contamination
   96, **97**
   fast food 50
   nutrition 50
   size 48–50, **49**
children
   food marketing 69
   obesity 22, **26**, 27, 31
   school meals 76, **77**, 111
China **15**, **22**, **31**, 73
chlorine 96, 97
cholesterol, LDL 33, 65
clean eating 120–1
climate change 80, 81,
   84, 86, 133
community 8, 130
community gardens 119
community supported
   agriculture programmes
   (CSA) 116, 117, **133**
compost 85, 88, 89
confectionary 17, **62**, **63**
contamination 90, 95, 99, **100**,
   106, 108 see also bacteria
convenience stores 40, **41**, 116
coral reefs 88
corn 70, 73–4, **75**, 76, **108**, 109
corn syrup, high fructose (HFCS)
   16, 17, 30, 62, 74
cortisol 44, 45
cover crops 70, 71, 86
COVID-19 **37**, 45, 100, **101**
cravings 53, 68
creation-based systems 133–4
crop rotation 70, 71, 86, 88, 107
culture and diet 41, 45

dairy foods **18**, 123, 124, 133
Dathal (DCPA) 90
DDT 106
death, causes 10, 32–3, 92, 134
decentralization 134
Deering, Amanda J. 100

deforestation **71**

delivery services **67**, 126, **127**

dementia 56–7

depression 57

developing countries 13, 15,
27, 31–2

diabetes 10, 11, 24, 31, 33,
35, 60, 134

diet *see also* nutrition; Western
diet

brain function 55–6

calorie sources 38, **39**

culture 41

effect on mortality 10, 134–5

emotions 41

flexitarian 123

food culture 45

intake levels **10**, 11

Mediterranean 121–3

nutrition **56–7**

plant-based 124–5

diet culture 131

discrimination, weight bias
23–4, 131

disease

antibiotic resistance 92

dietary effects 10, 19, 32–3,
134–5

factory workers 101

obesity 22, 24–5

in plants 71

salmonella 95–6

Dr Pepper 53

drinks *see* beverages

E. coli 98, 99, 100, 108

earthquakes 87

eating disorders 130

eating patterns 41–5

see also meals

ecosystem damage 19, 72–3, 80

education programmes 110, **134**

eggs 55, **96**, 97

emotions 41, 44, 57–8

endocrine disruptors 64

environment *see also* climate
change; pollution

biodiversity loss 18, 19, 70–1

erosion 88

monocultures 72–3

stewardship 105

European Union 12, 66, 75,
90, 92, 94, 97, **105**, 107

factory farms 12, 13, 28, 80,
93, 95, 101, 118

Fairtrade **104**, 105

farmers' markets 82, 83,
116, 134, **135**

farms *see also* agriculture

organic 107–9

size 12–13

subsidies 75–6, 105

traditional **12**, 71, 85–6

weather 74

fashion **24**, **25**

fast food

advertising **54**, 112, **113**

calorie information **59**

consumption levels 29

convenience stores **41**

delivery services **67**

development 29

globalization 18, **19**

reducing consumption 123

socioeconomic factors **38**, 40

Trump's choice of **30**, 31

fat acceptance 23–4, **25**

fat, body 35 *see also* obesity

fatphobia 131

fats, dietary

healthy sources 54

intake levels **10**, 11

partially hydrogenated
(trans) **10**, 11, 62, 65

saturated 32, 33–4

feedlots **48**, 92–3

fermentation technology 51,
110, 133–4

fertilizers 14, 84, 86–8, 107

fibre 52, 54, 60, 61, 123

fish **57**

fitness 25

flavour

bliss point 52, 53

local food movement 83

flexitarian diet 123

food assistance programmes
105, 110

food choices

crops 70–1, 124

nutrition 59–61

obesogenic environments
38–40

shopping 115

food co-ops 118, 119, 135

food deserts 38, 39–40, 116

food miles 82

food safety *see also* bacteria
herbicides and pesticides
89–91

ingredients 64, 65, 66

labour conditions 101,
105, **106**

recalls 98–100

food security 72, 73, 132, 133

fossil fuels 81, 86–7

fracking 86

free range 96, 97

fructose 17

fruit

contamination 90

nutrition **56**, 57

year round availability 81,
84, 85

fungi **70**, 71, 89

genes, weight management 25

genetically modified organisms
(GMOs) 89, 106, 107

ghrelin 60

globalization 31–2, 81–2,
84, 85, 94

glyphosate 89

GMOs 89, 106, 107

Green Revolution 14

greenhouse gas emissions 19

health programmes 110–11, 113

heart disease 10, 11, 16, 24, 25,
33–4, 65, 134

heartburn 44, 45

herbicides 89, 91

high fructose corn syrup (HFCS)
16, 17, 30, 62, 74

high-yielding varieties (HYVs) 14

hippocampus 57

Hong Kong **81**

hormones 60

hunger 60

hydro-fracking 86, **87**
hypertension 34

India 9, 16, 18, **19, 31**, 80, **106**
Industrial Revolution 11
ingredients
  bans on use 64, 65, 66
  processed foods **74**, 75
insecticides 15, 90, **91**
insulin 35, 44, 60
irrigation 88, 89
Italy 31

Japan **42-3, 81**, 116
junk food see also fast food
  brain function 56
  eating on the go 43
  organic 109

kale **57**, 90, 100, **120**
KFC 29, **40**, 41

labelling, legislation 112-13, 114
Lang, Tim 82
LDL cholesterol 33, 65
legislation see also regulations
  global need for 104-5
  labelling 112-13, 114
  organic food 107
  value systems 109-10
legumes 60, **61**, 107
leptin 17, **60**, 61
lettuce 95, 98-100, 108
lifestyle changes 131
livestock
  antibiotic usage 93-4
  farm subsidies 76
  organic **108**, 109
livestock feed 50, 74, 124, **125**
lobbyists 113, 114
local food movement 116
locavores 83

macronutrients 62
manure 85, 88, 89
marketing 67-9, 77
  see also advertising
McDonald's 18, **19**, 28, **29**,
  30, **31**, 59, **69**
meals see also eating patterns

communal **8-9**, 43, 130, 131
portion sizes 43
school meals 76, **77**, 111
solo dining 41-3
stress 44
meat see also processed meats
  antibiotic usage 93-4
  consumption levels 16
  consumption reduction 118,
  123, 133, 134
  contamination 96
  cost and industrialization 16
  feed required for production
  124, **125**
  income relationship 16
meat packing plants 101
medically-tailored meals 110, 111
Mediterranean diet 121-3
mental health 130
menus, calorie information **59**
metabolic health 17, 21, 25
Mexico 30, 76
monocultures 72, 73, **80**, 81
mood see emotions
mortality, causes 10, 32-3,
  92, 134
Moskowitz, Howard 53
MRSA (methicillin-resistant
  Staphylococcus aureus)
  92, 94

nitrogen 84, 85, 86, 88, 89, 107
North American Free Trade
  Agreement 30
nutrition see also diet
  education programmes 110
  food choices 59-61
  food labels 112-13, 114
  industrialization of farming
  48, 50-1
  macronutrients 62
  precision fermentation
  technology 51
  processed foods 17
  range of foods 71, 124
  saturated fat 34
  training of doctors 26

obesity
  childhood 22, **26**, 27, 31

definition 23
diet causes 30, 134
discrimination 23-4, 131
epidemic 131
global increase 22, 27-8,
  31-2
health risks 24-5, 35, 36-7
high fructose corn syrup
  (HFCS) 17
medical treatment plans 26
solo dining 42
obesogenic environments
  38-40, 54, 77, 127
oceans, dead zones 88
Oliver, Jamie 111
orexin **60**
organic food 105, **106-9**
orthorexia **120, 121**, 130

packaging 64, 66
palm oil 71
pancreas 35, 60
peaches 81, **83**
peanut butter 95
pesticides 14, **15**, 89-91,
  101, 106, 107
PETA **126**
pineapples **64**, 81
plant-based diet 124-7
plantations 71
plastics 19
policy makers
  effect on food environment
  18, 19, 76-7, 127
  global legislation 104
  value systems 109-10
Pollan, Michael 62, 63, 66
pollution 8, 19, 88
polyculture 70, 71
population growth 48, 49
portion sizes 43, 112
poultry 48-50 see also
  chickens; turkey
precision fermentation
  technology 51, 110, 133-4
prefrontal cortex 68, 69
preservatives 62-3
processed foods
  bliss point 52, 53
  convenience stores **41**

flavour **50**
growth of 28
health risks 51
nutrition 51, 52, 53
organic 109
reducing consumption 123
processed meats
cancer risk 17
intake levels **10**, 11
protein 54, 134
public health programmes
110–11, 113

ready meals 28
recalls 98–9
regulations
advertising 69, 77
antibiotic resistance 94
ingredients 64, 65, 66
opposition 113, 114
rice 70
RoundUp **89**

salmonella 94, 95–6, 97
salt **10**, 11, 34, 53
Samoa 32
satiety 17
saturated fat 32, 33–4
school meals 76, **77**, 111
seasonal food 81, 83
Seba, Tony 133–4
self-sufficiency 119
serving sizes *see* portion sizes
shelf life 51, 63, 65
Shoppers' Guide 90
shopping
active choices 115–20, 135
food deserts 39–40
supermarket layout **114**, 115
Slow Food 30, 31
social media 112, **113**, 120, **121**, **131**
socioeconomic factors 16,
39–40
soda taxes 30, 76
soft drinks *see* beverages
soil quality 84, 85, 88, 106
solo dining 41–3
soybeans 17, **72**, 73, 76, 106, **107**
Standard American Diet (SAD)
29–30 *see also* Western diet

staple foods 119
stomach, stretch receptors 61
storage 63
strawberries **80**, 81, 83
stress 44
stroke 10, 11, 25, 33, 34
subsidies 75–6, 77, 105, 110
sugar
cane production **71**
comparison of foods 52, **53**
confectionary **17**
daily recommended levels 113
diabetes 35
farm subsidies 76
intake levels **10**, 11
junk food **41**
metabolism 17
processed foods 53
soda taxes 30, 76
superbugs 91–2, 94
supermarkets **114**, 115
sustainability 132
sweetness, calorie
expectation 122
symbolism of food 8–9, 130

taste *see* flavour
taxation 30, 76, 77
trade deals 30, **96**, 126
'traffic light' system 114
trans fats, intake levels **10**, 11
transportation 81–2, 83
Trump, Donald 30, 31, **96**
turkey **16**, 17, 32
TV dinners 28

'ugly produce' programmes
116, 117
UK
advertising standards 69
ingredient use 64
public health programmes 113
school meals 111
ultra-processed foods 12, 123
urban farms **133**
urbanization 84
US Department of Agriculture
(USDA) 49, 90, **105**, 107, 110
US Food and Drug
Administration (FDA) 64, 100

USA
antibiotic resistance 92, 94
chlorine washed chicken
96, 97
corn production 73, **75**
eating patterns 43
farm subsidies 75–6
farming 12, 13
fast food development 28–9
food safety 97, 98–100
health programmes 110
ingredient use 64, 65, 66
marketing budgets 68
meat consumption levels 16
obesity 25
organic food 107
poultry size 49

vaccines 37
value systems 109–10, 135
veganism 126
vegetables 34, **35**, **56–7**, 90, 117,
122, **123**, 132
vegetarianism 16, 124–5

waste food 116, 117
water
irrigation 88, 89
livestock and dairy
production 125
pollution 8, 19, 88
weather 74, 81
weeds 89
weight bias 23–4, 131
weight loss 58–9, 131
Western diet
composition **10**, 11, 29,
34–5, 37
globalization 18, 19, 30–2
health risks 32, 56–7, 104, 134
wheat 17, 70, 76
White Castle restaurant 28, **29**
whole foods 60, 61, 66, 123
willpower 54
workers' health 101, 105
World Health Organization
(WHO) 14, 15, 17, 22, 27, 89,
94, 113
World Trade Organization 30, 32
World War II 49, 86

Acknowledgments:
This book would not have been finished without
the encouragement and help of my husband,
Dan Call. Many thanks to Jane Laing, Isabel
Jessop, Phoebe Lindsley, Tristan de Lancey
and the entire team at Thames & Hudson for giving
me the opportunity to write about one of the most
important topics there is: the global food system.
The COVID-19 pandemic has only heightened
my conviction that human health and the health
of our planet depend on reforming global
agriculture, trade and healthcare policies.

First published in the United Kingdom in 2021
by Thames & Hudson Ltd, 181A High Holborn,
London WC1V 7QX

First published in the United States of America
in 2021 by Thames & Hudson Inc., 500 Fifth Avenue,
New York, New York 10110

Is Our Food Killing Us? © 2021
Thames & Hudson Ltd, London

Text © 2021 Joy Manning
General Editor: Matthew Taylor

For image copyright information, see pp. 138–139

British Library Cataloguing-in-Publication Data
A catalogue record for this book is available from
the British Library

Library of Congress Control Number 2020951830

ISBN 978-0-500-29566-3

Printed and bound in Slovenia by DZS Grafik

Be the first to know about our new releases,
exclusive content and author events by visiting
thamesandhudson.com
thamesandhudsonusa.com
thamesandhudson.com.au